How
to make
work
FUN!

People must not do things for fun.
We are not here for fun.
There is no reference to fun in any act of Parliament.
A.P. Herbert
Uncommon Law

Bollocks
Roger Mellie, Viz Magazine

How to make work FUN!

An alphabet of possibilities…

David Firth

Gower

First published 1995 in hardback by Gower Publishing Limited

Paperback edition published 1998 by
Gower Publishing Limited
Gower House
Croft Road
Aldershot
Hampshire GU11 3HR
England

Gower
Old Post Road
Brookfield
Vermont 05036
USA

David Firth has asserted his right under the Copyright, Designs and Patents Act 1988 to be identified as the author of this work

British Library Cataloguing in Publication Data

Firth, David
How to Make Work Fun: Alphabet of
Possibilities ...
I. Title
658.3

ISBN 0-566-07712-4 (hbk)
ISBN 0-566-07647-0 (pbk)

Library of Congress Cataloguing-in-Publication Data

Firth, David, 1963-
How to make work fun: an alphabet of possibilities / David Firth.
p. cm.
ISBN 0-566-07647-0
1. Quality of work life. 2 Work – Psychological aspects. 3. Job satisfaction. 4. Work environment. I. Title
HD6955.F57   1995   94-47406
306.3'6 – dc20   CIP

Typeset in Novarese by FdK
and printed in Great Britain at the University Press, Cambridge.

Disclaimer

There are two lies in this book.

This is one of them.

By the Same Author

World Peace in a Fortnight!

Reconciling Moral Pragmatism within a
Non-interactive Dualism: A Thesis

The Meaning of Life –
A Brief Introduction in Old High Welsh

Handicrafts of Yesteryear: Fog Knitting, Water Plaiting,
Soot Juggling and Building on Sand

How to Make Work FUN! is the author's fifth book
and his most ambitious to date.

I'll say it before the critics.

There's nothing new in this book. No new ideas. Nothing that you won't have thought of yourself.

It's sad that the ideas in this book

– so obvious, so simple –

aren't actually being put into practice...

The day before I started writing this book, W. Edwards Deming, one of the most influential management theorists in the modern world, the Professor of Quality, the man who massively influenced the post-war industrial and economic miracle in Japan (because America wouldn't listen), died. Deming argued for decades (he was still lecturing in the last of his 93 years) that if you improve quality at source, then productivity will rise and costs will fall.

He also knew the dreadful waste inherent in treating human beings like commodities. He advocated ridding workplaces of fear and competition. He was talking about teamwork and customer care 40 years ago. We nod at his wisdom, but we are still failing to put it into place in our organizations.[1]

This book says 'Hello and thank you' to his ideas but also to the man, because W. Edwards Deming loved music, cats and fresh tomatoes.[2]

[1] See J if for Just Do It!
[2] See B is for Banalities.

Contents

Contents

Contents

Contents

Hi there. Welcome!

And congratulations: you've made it this far. There is a glimmer of hope for us all.

Just spare a thought for the legions of the terminally serious who came across this book in the book shop, saw the word

'Work'

closely followed by the word

'Fun'

and bought this book

IMMEDIATELY

just so they could go straight outside and burn this soppy, liberal, nursery school, right-brained, nonsense, left-wing waste of time, my people don't need fun, they need a job!!!!

Thanks for sparing a thought for them. I think I can hear the sirens now.

Well, reader, this book is being written by someone who is just like you. And, I suppose, like them (give them a wave as they are eased into their strait-jackets. Oops. Too late).

Because we are all in business. And we are, after all, here to make money, let's not miss the point. In fact, we are always looking for ways to make more money – that's why there's such a trade in management theories: TQM, JIT, BPR, TTFN. But those theories usually just work on the work. We cut it, we reshape it, we push and pull it, we measure it in every way we can imagine, we polish it and we make it nice and shiny. And that's how we justify our salaries: we work on the work. But unless we change the attitudes and behaviours of the people who actually do the work and fully realize their potential, building new fertile environments for them to do it in, then nothing much will have changed.

This book is based on a few core ideas. They can make more money for organizations by releasing the potential of the poor sods who are waiting for people like you and me to finish our work on the work, so that they can get on and do it.

Here are those core ideas:

1. Work's crazy.

2. Work's scary.

3. Work should also be fun.

What do I mean?

It's crazy!

We are asking our people to put in more and more effort in a world of fewer and fewer resources.

We need to release the creativity and commitment of these individuals if we are to get the best out of them, for the greater good of all concerned.

Happy people work more effectively, with greater creativity and commitment.[3]

Our organizations have not been the best environment in which to foster this creativity and commitment, because we have run them like schools.

Why schools? Well, what is a company's strongest weapon? Guilt.[4] What is its greatest inhibitor to self-expression? Fear.[5] What does it value most? Conformity.[6] What does all the weight of traditional management thinking imply – what do the very structures on which our traditional organizations are based, suggest? That people must be controlled to produce the best work. This is humbug management.[7]

---

[3] See P is for Proof.
[4] 'We gave you a job.'
[5] 'If you are not careful, you'll lose your job.'
[6] 'That's the way that job is done around here.'
[7] 'Fun? Bah, humbug!' Ebenezer Businessman.

Business has gone crazy. Being busier than we used to be just doesn't describe it. Disruption and change are the constants of life at work. Work is re-engineered, businesses go bust or are taken over. Innovation happens in a nanosecond, and technologies are arriving that develop the products almost as fast. People are having to change their self-concepts – the way they think about themselves at work in order to work smarter, harder, faster, to take more responsibility and to develop new skills. Even if humbug management brought us successfully from the Industrial Revolution to the last decade, business can no longer afford to behave in the old, slow, mean-spirited, controlled, traditional ways.

It's scary!

People used to be scared by their autocratic, humbug bosses. Although those bosses remain a problem, the workers of the current business environment have many other reasons to be just as scared. One of my clients described life at work as 'like a roller-coaster'. And he didn't mean the sales figures.

But, there is an unchartered area of motivation and liberation which revolves around a new truth for these tough times:

> *People have changed. They know more, they want to know more, they expect more, they want to be more, they want to fill up their lives with work that has meaning. There's no time to worry about keeping everybody in line. Control is an illusion only achieved when people are controlling themselves.*

Work *is* like a roller-coaster, and most of us don't have a choice about being on the ride. It is, therefore, scary. But the successful organizations of the future, those which will be getting the greatest creativity and commitment out of their people, will be giving them the other half of the roller-coaster thrill too.

That's why I call this uncharted area of liberation Fun.

Oh dear. That was all a bit serious. Forgive me. Let's try again.

Work should also be FUN!

We spend 41% of our lives at work. Since we spend another 30% of our lives asleep, we're not giving ourselves much of a chance for anything else.

So work is unavoidably a part of life. Yet if we approach life as an alternative to work, if we can only hope to separate and divide and not synthesize, if we have drained work of all that is enjoyable, what have we left? We find ourselves working in states of boredom, irritation, bitterness, frustration, confusion and guilt – and that is not a suitable environment in which to encourage optimum performance. How can we deliver excellent service, or manage resources and ideas better than our competitors, if we'd really rather not be at work at all?

We envy people who tell us that their work is fun – some artists, some waiters I've met, the Richard Bransons of this world, the list is not long – because their ability to achieve seems to be tied inextricably to their ability to enjoy their achievements. The two abilities feed or nurture each other, and that makes them perform better. The enjoyment is not something that can be earned only when the task is complete.

So this book is about how to introduce **life** back into **work** so that we can inspire people to **enjoy** the fast, fickle and frightening world in which we do business so that we can improve the bottom line **now**.

That will take change.

> ## Don't worry
> ## All things can be changed
> ## There are no rules

How can we change? By asking the Big Four Change Questions:

1. Why do we do things the way we do them now?
2. What if it were different?
3. Do we have the guts to do things differently?
4. What should we do?

This book offers at least 89 answers to Question Four, but first....

How to use this book

I've noticed that it is the fashion amongst writers of so-called 'self-help' books to offer, quite early on, alternative ways of reading the book itself – you know,

- by giving a skeleton view for quick reference, or
- by suggesting certain chapters that summarize key ideas, etc. etc.

I'm a slave to fashion, so here are some ways to use this book:

1. Well.
2. Badly.
3. As a hat.

Who should read this book?

Anybody who goes to work who wants to change it for the better.

If you have to manage anybody, if you have to lead a team or a whole organization, this book is designed to be a provocation. I hope it provokes you to think of the many substantial and the even more insubstantial ways[8] in which you could introduce more **life** into **work** in your company. You'll find tips, exhortations, exercises and stories from organizations like yours who are having **fun** and others who are not having **fun** at all.

If, on the other hand, you feel that you don't have enough say in the running of the organization to influence change personally, do the following:

1. Read **I is for Influence**.

2. Give this book to your boss. Or, better, go straight to the top. Leave it in the CEO's toilet. (Perhaps that is going straight to the bottom of the top.)

AND NOW, THE BOOK:

[8] See also B is for Banalities.

How to make work FUN!

An alphabet of possibilities…

A

is for

AAAArgh!

Attention

A is for...

AAAArgh!!

which is the word we utter when we need some fun. Other words could be:

OOOOhhh!

Whoah!

Gnnngggghhh!

(probably through clenched teeth)

and
Whattheheckishetalkingabout?!!

These involuntary and apparently meaningless sounds are produced in reaction to the first of the Big Four Change Questions (see page 5). Your brain is thinking:

'Why do we do things the way we do them around here?'

And it simply can't form a sensible answer.

The business world is full of these sounds, every day, up and down the country. And when we make a sound like that it makes us mad and sad and frustrated and unhappy and it makes us feel that we would really like to be somewhere else and...

AAAAAAAArgh!!!!

WARNING! WARNING!
Important point!
Hey, this one's for you. Yes you!
The one in the strait-jacket

If we really want to be somewhere else, we can't be being as productive as we should be. And if we aren't being as productive as we should be, that will lead to low productivity. And low productivity leads to low dosh, money, dough, bread, spondulicks. And then you get fired. And that's logic for you, Jim.

If you have uttered, or heard a colleague utter, **AAAAAAAAAAAAArgh!!** recently, then read on.[9]

---

[9]Words like **AAAAAAAAAAAAArgh!!** are also used as names by minicab firms and electricians in a desperate attempt to be first in the telephone directory.

A is also for...

Attention

To please people is a great step towards persuading them.
Philip Dormer Stanhope

From the cutting edge of child psychology (and that's sharp), some advice that might be usefully applied to management.

I listened to a radio talk show/phone-in programme. An exasperated mother rang to seek help: 'He's so well-behaved sometimes – I know he can be a good boy when he wants to be. It's just that he doesn't seem to want to be very often.' In the background, the boy in question wailed and shrieked. He seemed to be breaking things. The advice?

> *'Children crave the attention of their parents – whether that attention is in the form of a smack or a hug. Try this. Whenever your child misbehaves, do nothing. Remain totally neutral. Don't give him the attention he is demanding. But when he does something good, lavish praise on him. Make sure that all interactions with your child encourage, rather than forbid. Those interactions are too precious – for both of you – to be wasted on admonishment.'*

Do nothing? That takes guts...

Ignore the failures and cock-ups of your people? Wait only for the successes and give Unlimited Positive Response? Well, yes. Very nearly. Absolutely definitely almost. People do need to know what their cock-ups are, but only so that they can put it right next time. They do not need to be scolded.

One other piece of management advice from the same show:

> *'You can't love your child all the time. Don't pretend that you can. But you never have an excuse not to be interested.'*

is for

Balance

Banalities

Boredom

B is for...

Balance

When we think we know something there is something we do not know.

Christmas Humphries

white
hard   soft
male   female
self   other
success   failure
complexity   simplicity
focused   diffuse
certainty   ambiguity
active   passive
teaching   learning
intention   happenstance
analysis   intuition
control   autonomy
urgency   importance
cutting your losses   giving the benefit of the doubt
not rocking the boat   making waves
rolling your sleeves up & getting on with it   chatting at the coffee machine
travelling on to the next town   staying here to admire the scenery
artichoke heart & Parma ham   cheddar cheese & pickle
Mozart   Metallica
security   risk
imitation   innovation
left brain   right brain
competition   cooperation
logic   faith
cynicism   naivety
sprint   marathon
tension   calm
order   chaos
answer   question
oooh   aaah
open   closed
yin   yang
black

A Balance Sheet

The art is in the balance. When we settle in one place, we become immediately aware of its opposite. Why? Because life – or work, or life in work, or managing, or being managed – is all one system. We cannot separate or divide (although humbug management would tell itself otherwise) without implying all the things that are left behind. If we do, then we focus our powers on a lesser part of a greater whole. There is a cost in developing such imbalance.

Over Balance

Even this Taoist reflection needs to be balanced with the realities of running a business. How can we strike the balance between giving somebody freedom to act and ensuring that they act in 'the right way', based on our valuable experience? How can we nurture the corporate spirit and still make sure we get the money in? How can we balance the needs of the individual with the needs of the group (and The Group)? How can we delight in teaching someone everything we know without experiencing the fear of their taking over our position? How can we tell the truth and keep the job? How can we bring a light perspective to our work and at the same time demonstrate our discipline and respect? Can I answer these questions? Can you?

It demands an impressively flexible style-width to cope with all the shades of grey between the poles of black and white. Some people like to be told what to do. Others, needing freedom, will react against such direction. You have to balance your style with their needs, so that no one style, no one response, no one solution becomes dominant.

The tightrope walker makes constant minor adjustments to maintain balance as she walks across the rope. She *never* has balance – she has only the result of the last tiny movement. Before she even has the opportunity to say 'I am balanced', she has to seek feedback from her position in the environment and immediately make another tiny adjustment to compensate. She is constantly aware of the whole system. For her, 'Yes, I've got it, I'm balanced' comes just before the lonely plummet to the ground.

A *Balance Sheet* *Exercise*

Imagine that you could sell the business. You'd call in the FD, the accountant and the solicitor. You'd draw up something like a balance sheet, assets and liabilities and so on. You'd measure the overheads and count the pencils. You'd get an idea of what the business is worth. Then you'd discuss who'd buy it and how you'd negotiate the best deal.

Extra Balance

What's the rest of your business worth – its spirit, its faith, its compassion, its intuition, its innovation? Which experts would you call in to help value it? How would you lay out the balance sheet? How would you indicate depreciation? Who'd buy this part of your company? What would you be prepared to give away in the negotiation?

And when you buy your next company, or recruit your next team, or seek your next colleague – what's on the balance sheet? What are they offering in their business plan? What would you expect and what would you be prepared to put in? What could you afford to leave out?

Every day, we draw up a balance sheet. Think of the tightrope walker. What tiny adjustments can you make, what feedback can you give, that helps the whole move towards balance?

B is also for...

Banalities

We are the same only in so far as we are all different.

At work, we are managing paradox: we come to work to balance our individual needs in a group environment; we need to create highly personalized human relationships in a highly impersonal world of machines, computers, information and 'resources'.

The new culture required is one that recognizes that managers can in fact only manage the messages they send, not the people: people ultimately always manage themselves.

And people will manage themselves better by releasing their individuality and having fun.

They might choose to express that individuality by decorating their own space in a way that relaxes or refreshes them. Now this might be a problem for those of you who are aesthetically inclined. For every person who expresses individuality with a framed print by Degas, there will be another who's got a photo of the spouse and the three kids on holiday in Rhyl, or who wants a sticker of Garfield on the PC.

Let them. They matter. Don't be a snob.

If you wanted a team of cardboard cut-outs, why didn't you recruit them?[10] Life is crazy, business is crazy, you need to encourage diversity and eccentricity just to have a chance of keeping a hold on reality.

Whatever you do, don't lose that curiosity you had about your people on the day you met them in their first interview. That is the level at which you need to be managing your people. It is your duty to know and take advantage of the unique talents and instincts of your people.

(And what is Garfield Management? I don't know, but I'll bet it's fun. And probably involves a lot of pizza.)

[10]See also R is for Recruitment.

HOW TO MAKE WORK FUN!

More Banalities

Here's an exercise

At the next team meeting get everyone to bring an item – it could be a favourite photograph, personal memento, in fact anything at all. The only stipulation is that it must mean a lot to them. These objects are called 'A Symbol of Me'.

At the meeting, before the first agenda point, ask them to tell each other, in turn, about their object – its history, its importance, and so on.

Note:

- how everybody gets excited, crazy, passionate (or at least interested) about something
- how different the objects are.

And then

Count the times:

- the audience laugh
- the performers smile whilst telling.

That's all. And then you can get on to the really important work.

So what will that silly exercise have done for you? You'll have learnt two things:

1. How to change the atmosphere in a room by getting everybody laughing.

2. We are strange, complex beings living in a shifting and ephemeral world. These banal objects are the things to which we give meaning. They matter. These are the sorts of things that make people tick. Strange to think isn't it? (I'll bet nobody brings a copy of their contract[11]). The smart manager recognizes that life is built on mundanities and crazy choices, influences, decisions, and can change his or her style accordingly. It is humbug management to treat everybody the same.

---

[11]In the same way that the *Encyclopaedia of Famous Last Words* does not contain the entry 'I wish I'd spent more time at the office'.

B is also for...

Boredom

You get killed if you stand still.

My nephew Peter, teaching me to play Super Mario Brothers

Only very slowly could technology or economic forces exert such pressures for change as we take for granted. As for intellectual stimuli, these could hardly be strong in a society dedicated to the inculcation of routine and preparation for death.

J.M. Roberts *Shorter Illustrated History of the* World, Helicon, 1993.

Depending which political philosopher you believe, boredom is either a good thing because it brings about revolution (Inge) or a bad thing, because people will commit any act – even criminal ones – just to avoid it (Russell).

Either way, if your business feels a bit like the autumnal Egyptian empire – cultivating routine and getting ready to send people off to their deaths – then you may have a shock around the corner. It will either be in the form of a revolution – after which the liberated masses will have you up against the wall with a blindfold on and smoking a last cigarette – or they'll steal your company envelopes, because even that is more thrilling than just another boring day.

Fear boredom in the workplace

Ask:

Is it boring here?

and

What could we do to make it less boring?[12]

and if you are feeling very brave

Am I boring?

[12]See I is for Interesting.

HOW TO MAKE WORK FUN!

is for

Communication

Control

C is for...

Communication

Communication is not simple...and the revelation of its hidden complexity is one of the great discoveries of the twentieth century. ...One sure sign of this complexity is our ignorance.

Dr P. N. Johnson-Laird

I know you believe you understood what you think I said, but I'm not sure you realize that what you heard is not what I meant to say...

Anon/Everyone

If this were a book on communication, I would tell you that communication has two immutable laws:

1. That you are communicating all the time (in your words, in your tone of voice, your actions, your dress, your hairstyle, your presence, your absence).

2. That you cannot not communicate.

Furthermore, I would explain that communication is not just a process of sending messages, but also one of negotiating meanings, and as in any negotiation, the meaning you intend is not necessarily the one which your audience takes away with them.

Furthermore, these transactions – sending and receiving messages and negotiating meanings – all take place in a dark, shifting and murky place called The Pool of Complexity, where everything you say and do – every initiative you launch, every explanation you give, every appraisal you make, every time you say 'Thank you' or 'What can I do to help?' or even 'Yes' – is complicated by an almost infinite number of factors, such as expectation, attitude, prejudice, indigestion, boredom, cynicism, hunches, uncomfortable seating, history, values and beliefs, air conditioning etc.

In fact, communication is such a hugely important and fundamentally thought-twistingly difficult thing to do that I'd advise you to leave it well alone if it were not for the two immutable laws mentioned above.

Continuing Communication

All that you can do is try to communicate brilliantly.

How?

1. Think. Learn. Act.

2. Use communication to build your vision of how things could be: use it to build trust and a human face to your organization.

And how do you do that?

Test everything you say and do against the question:

'Did what I have just done add to or detract from the values of trust and humanity that I am trying to build here?'

The ideal you should be aiming for is an environment of talk – chatting to each individual in the organization, free from the inhibitors of status, ambition, envy, or fear. This will take time and much effort at being there – not so much MBWA (Management By Walking About) as MBTA (Management By Talking About). It will also take nerve and humility. It will involve you living the message that you preach. There is a piece of Native American wisdom which suggests that the value of your life can be summed up in two questions: 'Does your philosophy grow corn? Do you walk your talk?'

Well, does it? Do you?

Because it's not easy – it's going to involve facing many embarrassing situations where you call someone over so that you can sincerely tell – and hear – the truth.

If you can't walk your talk, they will think you are lying.

If you don't tell the truth, they will know that you are lying...(the rumour network is faster, more authoritative and accurate than you would ever want to believe).

**This page intentionally left blank
(but I can't remember why).**

regularly, to instil a con

Note: These are the words that I would use (does t
they may sound stilted. You may want to tailo

1. 'Is there anything I can help you with?'

2. 'Does anybody think I'm bullshitting?'

3. 'I've put a whiteboard up here where everybody in the team can see it. It's for jokes, cartoons, wise sayings, motivational lessons, sketches, welcomes and farewells, strange facts. It's called the "It Makes You Think Board". Just do it!'

4. 'Somebody said I should put this in a memo, but I thought it would be better to do it face-to-face so you can tell me now what you think.'[13]

5. 'How is your family/ hobby/ Symbol of Me[14] doing?'

6. 'Do you need more information to be able to do this job better?'

---

[13]The 'paper or face-to-face' issue: you are going to be asking for more and more feedback, and depending on the size of your company, much of it will have to be through paper-based channels – forms and questionnaires (or indeed electronic channels such as E-mail). They will be greeted with, at best, cynicism or, at worst, the bin (or the delete button) unless the reader believes that the writer: 1. will listen, 2. will act, and 3. won't mount a witch hunt. The way that you can prove these things is by telling and showing people the positive benefits that have ensued from the initiatives that have been inspired by their ideas in the past and by thanking whistle-blowers.

[14]See B is for Banalities.

[15]See point 4.

gs To Say

ication culture quickly.

nean I sound like a book?), but to you (or from you)
e messages to your own vocabulary and style.

7. 'You know we had that face-to-face memo meeting[15] a couple of days ago? Well I have to make final recommendations on that issue this afternoon — I thought I'd just ask if you have had any other thoughts about it since we met?'

8. 'I'm sorry; I don't understand all that technical language — just tell me what you really mean.'

9. 'I messed up badly this time, folks.'

10. 'Look, I know you feel strongly about this issue. If you don't mind, I'm going to take notes so that I can record your complaints as accurately as possible.'

11. 'Does anyone in this meeting feel that they are being steamrollered?'

12. 'Does anybody here know a good joke?'

13. 'There must be a better way to do this process. Any ideas?'

14. 'Help!'

15. 'Thank you.'

C is also for...

Control

Sell your cleverness and buy bewilderment:
cleverness is mere opinion, bewilderment is intuition.

Christmas Humphries

We have less control than we think outside work and more than we think at work. If you think that you are in complete control outside work, you are as mistaken as if you think that you are in complete control inside work.

Let

go.

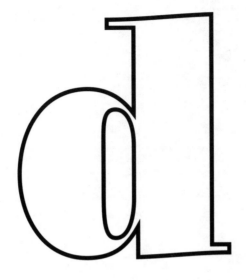

is for

Deflating Balloons

Delight

Dissatisfaction

D is for...

Deflating Balloons

Take every opportunity you can to deflate balloons, i.e. put things in perspective.

Note that there is a difference between deflating someone's balloon – letting the air out gently and considerately – and bursting someone's balloon which is a short, sharp violent act likely to induce cardiac arrest. Deflating a balloon also makes a funnier noise.

But if someone in the organization insists on posing with their mobile phone, give your team a set of imitation mobiles (you can get some marvellous models with batteries in them to light up the buttons and make 'realistic' noises).

If someone sends you a memo in pompous business-speak, send one back in Dutch. Or précis it (e.g. 'Do you mean "Let's have a chat"?').

One company I know, which was encountering real difficulties, awarded the entire Board new Jaguars. Great communication in tough times! Demoralizing to the work force? Absolutely, apart from one team, whose leader gave his colleagues toy replicas of the Board's motors. Every time a Director left the building to go to the car park, the team in question would bring out their cars and brrmm, brrmm, brrmm them across the floor.[16] Simple, silly, even childish, but better than experiencing depression.

At IBM, when the Big Brown really began to hit the fan, they would call

Perspective momentS

(subtitled: Let's Get It All In...)

when they would ask everybody to bring their favourite twig into work and show it in specially convened Twig Meetings at 10.35 a.m. on alternate Tuesday mornings.

Actually, they didn't do this, but I'm sure they would have felt better about losing all that money if they had.[17]

---

[16]It would, of course, have been even more fun if they felt able to share their joke with the directors concerned. But some parts of organizations change more slowly than others.

[17]See also S is for Silly.

D is also for...

Delight

Gooooooooooooooooooaaaaaaaaaaaaaaaaaaaaaaaaaaaaalllllllllllllllllllllllllll!

Jorge Curi

'Knock your socks off' customer service tells us to delight our customers. It makes sense, so we do delight them. And then, like penitents, we return to our drab caves where no customers enter. When do *we* experience a taste of that 'delight'?

For work to be fun it should appeal to all our senses and all aspects of our selves – especially in this world of diversity, colour, touch, pace, advertising, fashion, speed, style, and spectacle.

For entertainment your people might, in one night, watch on their satellite screens Brazil playing effortlessly beautiful football during the World Cup, followed by the digitally remastered *Snow White* on video.

They will eat out tonight at a Ghanaian restaurant, or at a Polish restaurant, if they want. Or they'll stay in and make a great sandwich out of Ciabatta or Mighty White.

The magazines they read on their way home will joke knowingly about Sartre, Warhol or sex.

On their fridge is a magnetic replica of Michaelangelo's David or an example of their child's latest finger painting.

The world excites, it sparkles. There's bags of choice and everything's packaged to please. We react to it by enjoying it and becoming eager for more.

Who said people are scared of change?

Fresh Delight

But does the office stimulate us in the same way? In at least three ways, we could bring delight to work.

Firstly, think what we do for customers: we decorate our public spaces beautifully – our board rooms demonstrate the delicacy of our artistic sensibility and the depth of our wallets. But our own spaces are not always delightful places to work.

Secondly, we will go to any length to please our customers – we reward people for extraordinary politeness, or if they've worked over the weekend to satisfy a customer demand. But do we go out of our way for each other? 'Don't make your customers satisfied,' we are told, 'make them raving fans!' But do we make raving fans of our colleagues?

Thirdly, we can 'liberate the emotional dimension of our psyche'. (Looking happy, I suppose). We just don't express our delight expansively.

The news that you've won a big account, or that you've saved a big account, comes into the office. Think of the range of emotions bubbling about under the surface at that moment – relief, gratitude, pride, elation.

Let it out. **Scream, hug, slap, cry, have an orgasm**. Whatever you feel. It's a roller-coaster!

'Oh, well done!' just won't do.

D is also for...

Dissatisfaction

I say it's a good thing to be dissatisfied. Dissatisfaction is a potent tool, used consciously, for bringing about change. Dissatisfaction is the pivot which can turn all the 'negatives' in this book – boredom, fear, guilt – towards a better way.

What are you dissatisfied with? Ask it in meetings. Here's the script:

> YOU: 'What can't you stand a minute longer? Come on. I can take it. Stop protecting me. All that inhibited tension is bad for (a) our company, and (b) your personal health. What have you been silently putting up with for too long now? What has driven you to breaking point? What has dissatisfied you so much that you've just got to make it better!!!!???!!!! Let it out.'

Stage direction: Pause and listen.

> YOU: 'Thank you. See, I didn't die. I'm still here. At least we all know where you stand now. Now we can think up a way to help.'

One of the key factors that stops work being fun is 'The Art Gallery Ballet',[18] a beautifully-executed dance of intricate interweaving where one dancer executes steps that almost but not quite brings him into contact with his partner.

For example:

Jill thinks she'd better not say what's bothering her because she thinks it's probably the most serious thing that Jane has ever had to deal with and she won't be able to handle it. Jane thinks she'd better not ask Jill what's bothering her because she thinks it'll be the biggest thing she has ever had to deal with and she won't be able to handle it.

Let it   out!

---

[18]Or, 'The Window Shopper's Quadrille'. Just watch people not touching as they carefully do exactly the same things.

HOW TO MAKE WORK FUN!

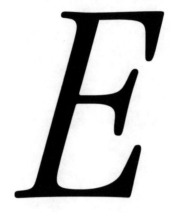

is for

Empowerment

E x 3

E is for...

Empowerment

Powerlessness corrupts. Absolute powerlessness corrupts absolutely.

Rosabeth Moss Kantor

For all those predominantly left-brained readers out there who are feeling a little giddy with all this touchy-feely stuff, thanks for staying with it this far. (By the way, that lightheadedness is caused by the oxygen of change.) Here's a reward for your patience.

This is a formula for productivity through empowerment:

Productivity (P) is a function of responsibility and authority and knowledge multiplied by success, divided by the negative effects of the environment, or for short:

$$P(f) \quad \frac{(r + a + k) \times s}{ne}$$

And that means, if you want an increase in productivity, you must make real, sincere and achievable input to the other side of the formula. So:

r = ask them to do it

a = let them do it

k = give them the tools to do it – train them

s = make it tough and achievable (and let them fail if necessary)[19]

ne = keep the negative effects of the environment – pessimism, fear, guilt, jealousy, rising damp – to a minimum. (If you don't, all the good work you've done on r,a,k, and s will be diminished[20]).

I'm sorry it is not any more complex, it just isn't. If you try to make empowerment any more complex than this, you are probably just trying to mask:

1. Your fear.   **2.** Your distrust of your people.

If 2 is the case, get new people. If 1 is the case, get out of the kitchen.

---

[19]Failure, or even asking for help, is not a weakness, but a necessary and unavoidable stage in constant improvement (see T is for Thanks). If you have someone who never fails, they may well be a genius, but they could just as easily be a coward.

[20]Do it too (see E is for E x 3).

E is also for...

E x 3

The Three Es of Leadership are:

Energy
Emotion
and
Example

People only change their behaviour when it is explained with passion and commitment and modelled to show the benefits of undergoing the change.

We have all grown up in a society naturally based on hierarchy – parents and teachers. We look up for leadership. If a leader did not exist it would be necessary to invent one. It is only when involved in humbug business that we notice that the leaders have stopped doing what the parents and teachers did – i.e. nurturing, developing and growing – and have replaced it with one narrow aspect of teacherhood and parenthood – control and discipline. We talk about Learning Organizations, but we should also be asking what teaching the organization could be doing.

So the rules of the Three Es of Leadership are:

- tell them what you'd like them to do, or better, what you would like to see happen;
- tell them why;
- don't ask them to do anything that you wouldn't do;
- tell them with passion – we are creatures of emotion, sensation and intuition as much as reason;[21] and
- live the message.

And when they do make the change, reward it, immediately, loudly, publicly. Send the message that these are the values that now matter in your organization.

[21]If it doesn't look as if it matters to you, why should it matter to them?

And now it's

Stop and Think Time.

"Hmm, those few pages have made me think...

...of a way I can adapt these ideas to use them in my organization.
Here's how:

....

...of someone with whom I ought to discuss these ideas.
Here's who:

....

...of a completely new idea that I've just had and which I'm going to implement.
Honest. Here's when:

....

...of something I once did that was great/embarrassing/empowering/hurtful.
Here's why:

....

...that it's a good idea I kept a receipt for this book as I may be able to return it to
the shop claiming that my senile auntie bought it for me."

The Inner R

In the 1970s, Timothy Gallwey and Bob Kriegel wrote a book called Inner Skiing. It was one of the first books I'd ever seen with two 'i's next to each other in the title, but the content was even more astonishing.

The book called the reader to understand — and I mean by that it did not teach, or advocate, or warn the reader — that the way to learn to ski was not by worrying about achieving the right technique, but by trusting the body to find its own best way to ski — just as we all find how to walk without a moment's thought for theory or method. Inner skiing means reaching for the 'perfect run' — that breakthrough moment when it all goes right and you feel peace on the mountain, grace under pressure. It's about taming that intrusive voice in our head that's saying 'mind that ledge; shift your weight here; put the pole in here'. We think the voice is helping but really it's obstructing by focusing on the problems rather than allowing us to experience the process. Inner skiing frees us from tension, rigidity and fear — the very things that take over when we try, try, try to get it right.

||er-coaster

Maybe work is an inner roller-coaster. It is fun and it is scary — just like the ski run — but the fun and fear are all part of the ride. And if we try too hard to tell ourselves how to ride the roller-coaster — 'scream here; clench your fists here; close your eyes here' — we will either miss the ride altogether or die during it (and I know people who seem to be trying their best to do both of those things).

The fun is in the experience — not in worrying about it beforehand or analysing it afterwards. Fun, a little word with big meanings, is a process, not a reward. But for some, fun is something that is deferred, perhaps until the weekend, perhaps until retirement age, perhaps, for some lost souls, forever.

Ride the roller-coaster in the moment. Don't judge, whinge or worry.

Feel the thrust of gravity, the shake of the car, the grinding of the metal, the shape of the wind. In these moments of simple awareness comes the feedback that allows us to experience the exhilaration of the 'perfect run' — whether on the slopes, in the roller-coaster or in our work.

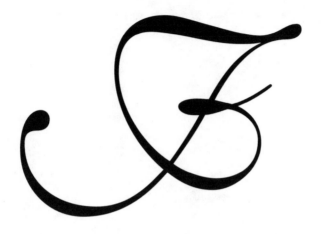

is for

Faith

Fantasies and Genies

**Fear, Guilt and all the other
outdated weapons of
humbug management**

Fool

F is for...

Faith

It is required you do awake your faith
A *Winter's Tale*, William Shakespeare

It is crucial. It moves mountains. Have it. Or do something until you achieve it.

Traditional, autocratic business is managed on the following assumption:

> # If you place ten adults in a room together and set them a task, then chaos will ensue.

This is a silly lie designed to maintain the power base and salary level at the top.

Yes, the ten need training and developing; yes, they need the benefits of leadership and cooperation and yes, it is true that there are going to be some who do not want to be liberated, who want to be told what to do.

But if we treat people like social deviants or mental cripples, we will, as sure as eggs is eggs,[22] find that they behave like them.[23]

And if your best efforts really have no effect on some individuals, then recruit new ones[24] – I am not advocating sainthood as a prerequisite for management. Just don't go round complaining that your people are stupid or lazy.

---

[22]And that's logic for you, Jim. And bad grammar.
[23]My thanks to Ricardo Semler, the visionary and non-conformist Brazilian businessman and author of the book *Maverick!*, for expressing this argument in front of a seminar of increasingly apoplectic respected British industry figureheads in London, September 1993.
[24]See R is for Recruitment.

F is also for...

Fantasies and Genies

What life at work is like for some people (your toughest customers):

- some fantasize about leaving to become a roadie for Metallica...
- some use the photocopier to reproduce their first novels
- some try to avoid contributing to leaving presents
- some use the phone for too many personal calls to arrange dates with lovers, discuss lovers, split up with lovers.

They are your toughest customers because they have never been told that there could be more to work than trying to escape it.

You'll have to try very hard to change this attitude. Appraise them regularly and be a genie. Ask them:

- 'What are your three wishes for making your life better at work?'

and

- 'What three things would you do if you were in charge here?'

and

- 'What are you going to do?'[25]

Tap into their potential by showing that there is more to self-actualization at work than using the free gym.

If they fail to take the bait, be rid of them. Look for someone who is going to offer more in your quest for corporate vitality.[26]

[25]See I is for In thine own eye.
[26]See V is for Vitality.

F is also for...

Fear, Guilt and all the other outdated weapons of humbug management

For example:

- 'You won't get anywhere in this company if you behave like that!'
- 'Why were you talking to that person?'
- 'Come in and close the door behind you.'
- 'Haven't you anything better to do?'

and all those other chilling and inhibiting phrases.

I hope that you will be measuring the eradication of these maladies through your new improved formal and informal appraisal systems.[27]

---

[27]See P is for Performance Appraisals.

F is also for...

Fool

We are tribal creatures. We fear expulsion from the tribe. That is why we have comedians – we join in laughter with the group at the expense of others. Through our laughter, we simultaneously expel that other and affirm our membership of the group. As long as people are not laughing at us, we are safe.[28]

The courts of medieval society recognized this. How better to prevent exclusion and guarantee safety than by having a permanent subject of laughter on the pay roll? Let's get the court fool in here!

But the fool is more than a professional entertainer. The king needs advice – who can he ask? His bishops? His knights? His noblemen? No – all these are practiced in the social arts of flattery and politics and deceit, and they all want something from him. The fool has nothing to gain and nothing to lose. What else will he tell but the truth? And how his truth will show up the lies and selfishness of the rest!

In short, the fool made things very difficult for those around him at court. Far from making them feel cosy and safe as part of the group, he had the liars and the bureaucrats and the fearful standing on the edges, looking like idiots...

If you already employ fools at work, celebrate! You've got a chance to hear the truth, an opportunity to see things in their true light. If you need fools, call a Fool Day:

- ask for a volunteer
- charge him or her with The Fooling Task: to walk around and publish a challenge to management, completing this question: 'This may sound foolish, but why don't we...?'.[29]

RULE 1: don't mistake fooling for whingeing.

RULE 2: don't take it personally, they may be trying to help.

RULE 3: management to respond within 24 hours.

---

[28]I believe this to be one of the top three primal fears along with the fear of death and the fear of being trapped in a lift with Loyd Grossman.

[29]You'll be surprised how sensible people become when they are allowed to be foolish. This suggests that the status quo must already be pretty daft...

Bigger Fool

And then, next month, let management have a go.

The biggest challenge with The Fool Day is getting the fool to feel safe. How does the fool know that management won't remember all this come the next round of redundancies?

I have seen MDs swear blind in seminars that they will welcome feedback and even criticism. I have seen them beg to be believed when they say that they will not hold anything against their people. And I have asked their people if they believe them, if they feel that they could walk into their MD's office on Monday morning and say that the MD is wrong. Those people have usually said 'Yes', but their eyes show that such trust will take more than words. Even seeing the MD sign a contract in blood will not do it.

So, what's the answer? How do we build that trust? How can we ask for honesty and openness and yet protect ourselves from hurtful criticism? How can we ask for the truth and still use the power of our position to cover our occasional mistakes, change our minds when it suits us and enjoy the privilege of forcing through decisions just because we say so?

The answer is, we can't.

Don't sack people who tell the truth.

- Explain to those who are mistaken.
- Help those who are confused to understand.
- Argue until at least you agree to disagree.

But don't sack people who tell the truth.

Period, as the Americans say.

1. Commit to increasing the energy with which you work ten-fold. For example, walk into the office with a bigger spring in your step (rather than slinking in straight to the coffee machine). Smile more (look people in the eye). Involve yourself in meetings with greater commitment. In everything you do, pump up the energy. Treat work like aerobics.

2. Tell someone how important their job is (to you, the company, the country – whichever is most accurate). Then prove it.[30]

3. Celebrate a success with somebody. Commiserate with someone on something that could have gone better. Look them in the eye and mean it.

4. If you see somebody hiding behind a mask (of bullshit, shyness, bureaucracy, or dull behaviour), help them to drop it. Say, 'Come on: what do you really feel?' Because sentences beginning 'I feel...' can **never** be wrong.

5. Look out for people feeling proud. Recognize it. Tell them you saw it and that it made you feel good to see it too. Say, 'I'm proud of you'.

---

[30]This is a tough one. If you are thinking 'How?' that's probably a sign of how necessary it is for that person to have it proved to them.

6. Welcome mistakes and questions. Obliterate fear and guilt. If someone screws up, say 'Thanks; that's given me a great idea on how [as appropriate]:

   (a) we can do that sort of thing better'

   (b) I can improve the way I tell people like you how to do that'.

7. Buy everybody in your team a sticky bun.

8. Remember (or find out) what the Symbol of Me (see B is for Banalities) is for three of your people, and ask about them.

9. Go to a book shop at lunchtime, browse along the Humour section and bring back a joke, a cartoon, or an urban myth. Better still, bring back the books themselves and leave them around. Encourage your people to read them, during work hours.

10. Invite a senior executive in to ask for his or her help or to show how well things are going in your team or area. Do the inviting on the phone, in full hearing of your colleagues.

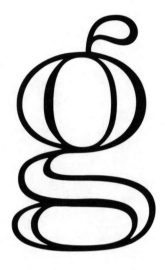

is for

Guts

G is for...

Guts

Courage is resistance to fear, mastery of fear — not absence of fear.
Mark Twain

Guts, as in

It takes guts to tell somebody that they ruin your day, or that the way people in the company interact at the moment wastes everybody's time and potential.

It takes even more guts to realize that you can manage your own destiny. If you want fun at work, fight for it.

- Imagine (how things could be better).
- Influence (reach the people who could make a difference).
- Convince (give them a sense of certainty, through the example of your own conviction).
- Sell (help them to buy your message, and to sell it on to others).
- Network (find other suppliers and make alliances).

It's like marketing a product from a company called Self, except that the product's not widgets, it's Fun. You're in charge.

and also as in

Gut feeling, which is one of the most beautiful expressions of the human desire to make sense of people and relationships.

This Friday evening, after work, I'll take up my God-given role as CEO and Chairman of a large company: Me. I'm managing a huge resource – my time. I manipulate it and create amazing byproducts with it. I'm the only supplier to the my-time market and I'm also one of the big customers, desperate for quality from his product. So I work hard at it. I put much effort into achieving maximum return from my investments.

Fresh Guts

This Friday evening I'll be deciding which film to see at the cinema and what kind of food to eat afterwards. I'll research and ask advice, but I know that what will happen is I'll eventually trust my own judgement – my gut instinct. And it will feel great. I'll trust it and it will give me an energy that will convince my friends.

If we try to negotiate the cinema or the restaurant, we will be lost.

As I get older I am struck more and more by how...
it is the intangibles that matter most – personality, culture, ego.

Felix Rohatyn, Financier (and that's a financier speaking...)

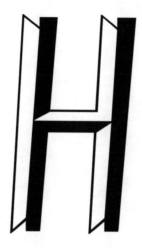

is for

Happiness

Honesty

How To Do It

Human

H is for...

Happiness

Happiness is a feeling you acquire, not a resource that you are born with. Happy people (ask one and see) are not lucky people. They do not have better experiences in life – they make better interpretations of their experiences. And this does not mean that happy people are simply positive thinkers. Their happiness comes not from the fact that they see the positive or good side to any event, but from the fact that they have made the choice. They have decided to see the positive or good side of things. Furthermore, happy people have decided not to think about the negative or bad side.

We all have these choices available to us.

Similarly, happy people seem to prefer frequency to intensity. Many of us feel that now is not the time to be happy, that the time for happiness is in a different place, or with a different group of people. Or maybe we store up all our happiness for One Big Happy Time, when it will feel absolutely amazing. Maybe that time will be at the weekend. Maybe that time will be when the holiday starts. Maybe that time will be this evening with the children. But then we find that it rains, or the children are ill, or the car needs repairing, or that we have to work at the weekend. And so we have to put that opportunity for happiness off to another time.

Happy people look for opportunities for happiness in the present, by concentrating on what is going well or how hard someone has tried; by focusing on principles defended or values asserted. They take their happiness in chunks, regularly.

Call them daydreamers if you want, but whatever happens, don't let them make you unhappy.

Greater Happiness

If someone close to you has died, you have a right to be unhappy. But if things are going badly at work, you've got a better chance of putting them right if you feel happy (positive, charged, energized) rather than wretched (deathly). Snap out of it. Stop being so selfish. Stop wallowing. You don't have much time.[31] Hands out – slapped wrists. There. Now: change your view: say out loud:

'Even though life seems pretty awful at the moment, and I know I'm supposed to look miserable just to prove to everybody else how serious this is, I'm going to pause for a moment and ask myself:

- Doesn't X still love me...and shouldn't that make me feel good?
- Don't I think that Y is the best piece of music ever written and as soon as I put it on, I know it will send shivers down my spine...and shouldn't that make me feel good?
- Wouldn't I begin to feel better if I stopped sulking and picked up that book from my Fun Toolkit...and shouldn't that make me feel good?
- Aren't I really good at Z...and shouldn't that make me feel good?
- Isn't the intensity of this challenge simply a reflection of the responsibility that has been placed on me and the confidence that someone has in my abilities...and shouldn't that make me feel good?
- Haven't I been through moments like this when things seemed just as impossible and didn't I come through even though I can remember *knowing* that I never would...and shouldn't that make me feel good?

and

- Just why do I think that I'm the centre of the universe?'

---

[31] 41% + 30% = not much time left (see p. 4).

　　　　　　　　　　　　　　　　　　HOW TO MAKE WORK **FUN!**

H is also for...

Honesty

*I never give 'em hell. I just tell them the truth
and they think it's hell.*

Harry S. Truman

Honesty is the oxygen of organizations...

There are very few evil people in our organizations who are withholding information or telling sadistic lies for pleasure. They are more likely to be afraid.

They need as much help and handholding in letting accurate information go as the most withdrawn, unambitious team member does in asking for it.

H is also for...

How To Do It

GAME 1

Right, what you do is everyone writes down on little pieces of paper the names of people. They don't have to be alive. They don't have to be famous – just known to the people around you. They can be fictional if you want. Write down as many as you can. Then fold up the pieces of paper and put them in a big pot. Then divide into two equal teams. The idea is that each person has to pick out a piece of paper from the pot and describe to his or her team mates the person who is named on it so that they can guess who it is. You can't use the name, or spell it out, or play charades. You have to do as many as possible in one minute. Then the other team has a go and the game proceeds until all the names are gone.

GAME 2

Right, split into two teams and write down as many common sayings or phrases as you can on the cards and then put them in a box. Then pick a card from the box at random and draw what comes to mind when you look at what's written on it. And your team mates have to guess the word or phrase that you are drawing. Then the other team goes and we carry on until all the cards are gone.

[32]'Oh Claire, the moment I met you, I swear...' Gilbert O'Sullivan.

How To Continue Doing It

The thing about 'how to do it' is that the how to do it almost always sounds unattractive. It doesn't sound much fun. It almost always sounds like we are not going to enjoy it. Or that it's going to be too complicated to bother doing. Or that it's going to be too simple to bother doing.

This is certainly true of the two games described above. And yet, I have never known any games to be more successful at getting people involved and making them laugh. They are dead certain, sure fire party hits. Guaranteed.

The fun isn't in the rules, it's in the doing. Every one of us has to become involved – whether it's carrying out the task, managing it, or becoming involved in the spirit of it.

And if we don't participate in the games, we have to question why we are at the party. If we are involved, and it still isn't fun, then we can change the game, or play another.

But at work, there should be no prizes for sitting back and telling us all it isn't going to work, or it isn't going to be worthwhile. At my party, you wouldn't even get a cheesy niblet.

H is also for...

Human

If an organization has no vitality, if it allows people to come to work and leave their personalities at the entrance, if it attempts to suppress individualism and eccentricity, then it will be developing people who are not fully human, but who are sub-human.

Here's a list from a big and very famous merchant bank, describing six touchstones for being a human manager at work. This list becomes increasingly important the higher up the organization one goes:

1. Anti-apartheid ('We are all equal').

2. Get the teas in ('We all help').

3. Shovel your own shit ('You're never too senior').

4. Be humble ('Be humble').

5. Be interesting ('The work might not always be interesting, but we can be').

6. Relax; be natural ('Be yourself').

i

is for

Imagination

Infection

Influence

Interesting

In Thine Own Eye

Intuition

I is for...

Imagination

Imagination rules the world
Napoleon

You'll need plenty of imagination to find new ways of motivating and entertaining your people. After all, your people's attention span and (despite what you might hear to the contrary) their resistance to change have been dramatically reduced by their experience of the speed and intensity of the information age.

There are all the usual sources of new ideas: the papers, the library, flicking through the latest management book in your local book store, and the way to test the validity of the ideas you find is by asking yourself the simple question:

> *'Hmm, I wonder what impact this idea would have on Fred (or other team member picked at random) if we did that in our organization?'*

The next step is to ask Fred.

Another method for creating positive alternatives is to hold

Imagination Brainstorms.

Call a group of people together and, for 30 minutes and no more, with no holds barred, push the group to produce the craziest, most extreme, most fantastical alternatives or solutions to a particular problem. It is a game in which the only rules are wild innovation and thoughtless 'silliness'. Encourage staid thinkers with a suitable forfeit. Record everything. And peruse the results at leisure for the gems. If nothing else, you will receive hundreds of different perspectives from which to review your problem.

Ten years ago you would have been thought crazy if you'd said General Motors would one day be offering a credit card. But that crazy person has given General Motors a new lifeline. It is that sort of crazy idea that you'll be needing now.

Two hints on things imaginative:

1. Keep doing them, even when times are tough.
2. Persevere with your people: a slow start to any project or initiative is not the same as failure.

I is also for...

Infection

Good vibes are contagious.
Jeremy Coleman, TGIF

...so get sick.

It is easy to be cynical about the touchy-feely side of business, all the soft, squelchy parts of work. Cynicism is like our white blood cells, protecting the body from invasion.

I've found that allowing people to enjoy the experience of fun is the only way to break down those barriers, to conquer those white blood cells. You catch them off guard – you attack them where they are least expecting it. There they are thinking you are going to show why they must loosen up, when all of a sudden you pull out your trump card. You:

1. involve them in a team building game,[33] or

2. give them a joke book to write a report on, or

3. give them a Polaroid that you took that shows just how silly they look when they are concentrating hard.

Encouraging them to enjoy themselves is hard work and needs patience and resilience. And if, in the end, you fail and they remain immune, then you have to question what else people like this protect themselves from – for example, change, adventure, or risk.

There are some people who never become sick.

Some people are so healthy it's spooky…

[33]Why do we only ever play these games – games that are designed to stimulate us, to solve differences and to make us think creatively – in the training room?

HOW TO MAKE WORK FUN!

I is also for...

Influence

Organizations change in units of one.

Peter Sole

Organizations do not change by:

1. Telepathy
2. Initiatives or strategies.

They change by people communicating with each other – talking and listening – and by people copying the behaviour they see other people exhibiting around them, once they have perceived a benefit to themselves in doing so.

It is therefore true that anybody, whatever level, rank or seniority they may be, can influence change (of whatever scale) in the organization.

If you look depressed or angry, you will affect the environment and the emotions of people around you.

If you preach vision and optimism, but display cynicism and envy, you will influence the environment and the emotions of the people around you.

If you talk about learning, but you've never faxed a colleague with an interesting and pertinent business article (or a thought-provoking cartoon), you will influence the environment and the emotions of the people around you – but you won't encourage learning, you'll encourage hypocrisy.

If you act harmfully in such ways with persistence and energy, your colleagues will eventually copy the bad behaviour, and make it a sad reality for the culture of your organization.

If you want to change the company, start with yourself.

Make **INFLUENCE** a core competency of the job.

> **Consider, measure and reward your people for the influence they have on their colleagues. What values of the culture do they make real in their behaviour, every day? Thank them publicly and loudly, for doing this. Show others how it is supposed to be...**

to do if you are trappe
And you can't leave to

1. Join the Fun Internet

Seek others. Meet with others. Share with others. Learn from others. Teach others. Laugh with others.

Exercise your fun muscles with like-minded people (there are at least two of us already).

In other words, do everything you can to keep your flame alive, because (since you've cared enough to read this far) you should know that the flame is more important and lasting than your current environment. You'll need the energy you obtain from the Fun Internet to be fresh and nourishing, to keep your soul free and to give you the bravery to fight the fight from within your fun-less environment.

hings

fun-less environment
our dream elsewhere.

2. Be a guerrilla

- Send anonymous e-mails.

- Blu-tack graffiti to the toilet walls.

- Send copies of books and articles that describe how you think it should be (or items you've written yourself) to the CEO's home address.

- Use your bad experiences to learn and develop your sense of how things should be (after all, one day you may be a consultant, or an author. It will certainly stand you in good stead when you look for a new company to work with).

- Steal pencil sharpeners (ultimately futile, but strangely satisfying).

I is also for...

Interesting

Come on, Steve!

Alex Higgins

B-is-for-Boredom's sprightly cousin.

Ask

'What's interesting around here?'[34]

I don't mean what's the gossip or what's titillating, but what's interesting?

Interest is a word derived from two Latin words – *inter esse* – meaning 'to be between'.

So a sure way to find out what's interesting at work is to find out what's happening in all those fundamental transactions between human beings, and between human beings and their products, that are the heart of all business.

Who has:

- discovered something?
- made something new?
- made a sacrifice?
- been heroic?
- made us feel proud?
- been courageous?
- made us laugh?
- got angry about something?
- had a great idea?

[34]Or, 'What's interesting about me?'

I is also for...

In Thine Own Eye

Workers educate. Managers act.

Chris Argyris

Participation is one of the keys to making work fun but to be truly fulfilling it needs to be active rather than passive. We each need to do more than simply be allowed to take part. The roller-coaster is not much fun if you never get past the ticket booth.

A quest to demonstrate the value of participation, to release the potential of people in the workplace, often begins with an honest and brave audit of the attitudes within the company.

Management asks people for information about faults in systems and practices that they now admit they might have been too blind and timid to recognize up until now. Now they have seen the light, they swear that they are willing to listen and, even better, to act! And so they have the audit, the staff survey, the team feedback.

Ten years ago this would probably never have happened and we should be grateful for progress.

But think of the thoughts underlying these events. No matter how well-intentioned the feedback is – and I have seen enough audit reports to know how much some people appreciate being given the opportunity to give their ideas on what is wrong – the roles and responsibilities in these surveys follow a distinctive pattern:

> 'We've told them what to do for long enough – now it's our turn to listen!'

and

> 'It's about time management did something – just wait!'

In fact, a survey based on these assumptions is working against participation – it is reinforcing the 'us and them' valley that it is designed to bridge.

In Thine Own Other Eye

Before the survey we had a one-way communication – boss to worker. Clearly outmoded in a crazy, shifting world; clearly demotivating for both parties. And that has been replaced with what? Two sets of one-way communication – worker tells boss what's wrong, boss moves to put it right and reports his actions. And everybody feels that they are coping with change.

What is needed is a two-way exchange – another side to the contract.

Each audit should explicitly ask all respondents what they (or they and their colleagues in their department or team or division) could do as their part in the improvement and how to track progress.

Just as companies who have put themselves through customer satisfaction audits often find out that their customers are surprisingly helpful and constructive, we might find that our managers are delighted when we take the initiative and move the desk, or order the extra telephone from supplies, or arrange a programme of cross-training.

If we as participants in the organization don't take the initiative, we are practising sub-conscious disempowerment. We are reinforcing the 'us and them' – 'I'm not going to take it upon myself to empower myself – it's my manager's job to empower me. And I'm going to sit right here until I am empowered. And in the meantime I'm going to whinge about not being empowered...'.[35]

Ask not what your company can do for you.

Ask only what you can do for your bloody self.

[35]See L is for Liberation.

I is also for...

Intuition

The intuition is the light which illuminates the intellect.
Unless there is intuition the light will no more be seen than
electric light in a socket of a lamp which has no lightbulb.

Christmas Humphries

Designed out of the objective world of measurement and risk-avoidance, intuition is the poor cousin of our rational mind. Although its burning, intense qualities have shaped the careers of some of the greatest inventors, leaders, even salespeople, I'll bet 'intuition' is a word you've never seen in a proposal, and therefore never seen acknowledged in a balance sheet.

A recently promoted sales manager speaks:

'One of the rewards of my new position was responsibility for supplier partnerships. This meant, as an ex-sales person, I now had the privilege of being sold to by our own suppliers. As these pitches progressed, I began to realize that, sometimes, I could hear a voice inside me saying "bullshit" – warning me when I was being spun a lie. I just wanted to say "Oh come on, just tell me what the real point is – don't give me the spiel". But my boss doesn't work like that. He has the sense too, but he prefers to play games with the salesperson. He'll wait one, maybe two whole meetings, gathering information, assessing risk, checking that he feels OK that he is being lied to, sifting through different responses, patiently awaiting his opportunity to trip the salesperson up with a sharp question or a sarcastic put down. And of course, in the end, he does – he has to, because he is being lied to. But it all seems a rather ridiculous dance. Why do we have to wait so long? I haven't got the time...'

'Typical men's head games' said another friend.

Intuition is a tool in our repertoire. We could make better use of it, if we didn't want to shackle it to numerical arbiters of worth.

But like creativity, intuition has to be cultivated and encouraged – it can't be switched on and off. Like laughter in the workplace, we must learn not to be suspicious of intuition.

J

is for

Job Title

Just do it!

J is for...

Job Title

Ignore it. It is not a constraint nor is it an alibi.
At best it is simply a signpost.

Peter Sole

Since we are trying to throw away what we are used to, undermine what makes us feel safe and treat ourselves less seriously, let's have a go at an old adage, the Job Title.

Like much in the complex world of work, this is difficult. Like the key to the executive toilet, the job title may turn out to be a shiny badge of status, a rung on a ladder which no longer exists, a tasteless souvenir from our visit to Career World. You spend your days striving for it and then once you've obtained it you spend your days striving for the next one. You buy it, and it buys you.

All hail, Macbeth! that shalt be vice-president hereafter.

Shakespeare

Those witches knew it

And maybe if we change a few job titles we might deflate a few balloons. We may even redesign some jobs accordingly. Here are a few ideas for alternative job titles:

- President of Vice
- Money Monkey
- Customer Interface Operative
- Environmental Recharger

But, even better (and what's the refrain?), let your people choose their own.

Another
Job Title

You'll receive some good, creative, light-hearted ones eventually – but you may spend a few days blushing at the sarcastic descriptions of what people think they actually do:

- Poor Schmuck who keeps the Almighty from running late

- Shit-taker in-chief

- Keeper of the Lies

- Head of Creative Accounting with special responsibility for corporate self-delusion

But what's the refrain?

All feedback is an education...

If your people truly think that these are the best descriptions of what they do, imagine what it is doing for their self-esteem, and their level of motivation.

J is also for...

Just Do It!

*The trouble with Freud is that he's never had to play the
old Glasgow Empire on a Saturday night
after Rangers and Celtic have both lost.*

Ken Dodd

Just do it! A battle cry for anything

There is a model for change which looks like this:

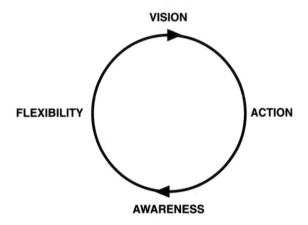

The model says that:

1. you need to know what you want to achieve
2. you need to do something
3. you need to be aware of the result your action is producing
4. you need to be flexible with your actions to adjust them until they produce the results you had imagined in your vision.

It is a simple model and could be adapted to anything, from moving yourself out of a chair to moving Mega Inc. into the next century.

But it is useless unless you take action.

Just Do It Again!

All the planning, analysis, self-awareness and education in the world will not help unless you bring them into the real world by taking action. Action is the only benchmark against which we can measure our development.

Encourage the energy and reality of **action:**

1. Celebrate success and thank well-intentioned failure.
2. Demonstrate that asking for help is not a sign of weakness but a way to improve.

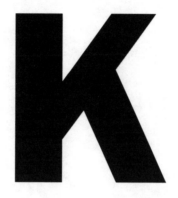

K

is for

Keep In Touch

K is for...

Keep In Touch

Wouldn't it be a good idea to drop a note to one of your people who, for whatever reason, you had not been able to say 'hello' to, face-to-face, recently?

Yes, it would.

Depending on your relationship with the person in question, you should watch the 'meaning' of such a communication. Imagine the thoughts that would pass through the mind of the lowliest wire-cutting operative when he gets a quick note from Sir Hugely Important And Not Usually Seen Around Here, his Chairman, saying 'Hi Bob, what are you doing?' However, you should persevere until this sort of informal, friendly, harmless, low-level KIT (Keeping In Touch) becomes a usual and even natural part of life at work.

And what about KITs for your external customers and suppliers?

- Don't wait for the organization to send out the corporate Christmas card.
- Don't wait to speak to your client until your team has missed a deadline.

Ring them up and say 'Hello, I...

- have some good news on a great new initiative we are running here'.
- have had a great idea on how we could cut down your invoicing time'.
- would like to fax you this fascinating article I've just read in the trade press'.
- was wondering what you think we could do better for you next week'.
- thought you might like to hear this great saying that one of my team mates put up on our "It Makes You Think Board"'.[36]

---

[36] See C is for Communication.

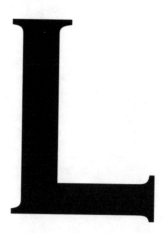

L

is for

Language

Laughter

Learning and Teaching

Liberation

Listening

L is for...

Language

KENT: *Where's the King?*
GENTLEMAN: *Contending with the fretful elements;*
Bids the wind blow the earth into the sea,
Or swell the curled waters 'bove the main,
That things might change or cease.

King Lear, original version

KENT: *Where's the King?*
GENTLEMAN: *Outside.*

King Lear, modern version

Language can make you see. It can make you laugh and cry. It can bring hope or despair. We know the emotional and practical effects of great speeches given by people like Martin Luther King and Winston Churchill.

But what are the effects of the language we use in our organizations? Not the language of the rhetoric prepared for corporate rallies or promotional literature, but the language used on the job every day?

The language we use is a reflection of the way our brains have been programmed. Does the language used in your organization nourish an environment of success, creativity and optimism? Does it always encourage action? Does it seek liveliness by seeking variation, peculiarity and distinction?

Or is it hackneyed, dull, cynical, pessimistic, encouraging only procrastination? Does it seem to reduce everything to uniformity and approximation?

Another Language

The English language contains half a million words, yet even the most erudite among us uses routinely only about 10,000. The average person uses 3,000 habitually. If your organization uses a similarly restricted vocabulary, it will hardly be surprising if its challenges, problems, events and successes all feel the same.

Push meetings to expand or change the language of business. Look for metaphors and similes that raise

1. a smile and possibly
2. a new idea.

Constantly challenge people to adopt a different perspective on the same old problems. Refer to work in non-work, leisure terms:

- 'This is like King Lear, Brian.'
- 'Running this project feels a bit like steering a wonky trolley at the supermarket, folks!'

Listen out for words that are continually used but betray apathy and laziness, and encourage experimentation with words that suggest variation, for example:

'I feel...[positive)
exhilarated/curious/captivated/enthralled etc...[negative]
in need of stimulation [for bored]
at full stretch (for too busy]
challenged (for worried]
I really want to stick the knife in [for I'm a little concerned].'

L is also for...

Laughter

I was at Hazlitt's marriage, and had like to have been turned out several times during the ceremony. Anything awful makes me laugh. I misbehaved once at a funeral.

Charles Lamb

I was invited into a company special event and after dinner there was an exercise to put on skits about life at work in this particular company. I thought this was an excellent, open and provocative idea. Everybody was able to see the light-hearted side of the company and its key players, its relationships and rituals; they had listened and observed. And now they performed. They presented these skits for the benefit of themselves and all the company – an entertainment, a diversion, holding a mirror up to reality. And the audience roared with laughter. They said 'this is extraordinary; look at the detail of the observation – and most of all, see how absurd we are made to look in our daily efforts! These people are not exaggerating! This is not a pantomime – this is the way we are!' They laughed and wondered and resolved to learn.

I returned the next week and everybody had stopped laughing. They were in the same ridiculous drama but had lost the perspective. Last week they watched their working lives reflected as a Feydeau farce. Today, back in the work, they were living a Kafkaesque tragedy. Nobody was able to see exactly the same conversations or behaviours that made them laugh last week as being funny today.

Funny isn't it?

Carry on Laughing

It only makes me stronger in my suspicion that the Frankenstein work we have created for ourselves – grave, fearsome, awe-inspiring in the worst sense – is somewhat feeble. Maybe the work can't stand it if we take it too lightheartedly.

What is it about work that makes us so pompous?

Laugh at work. Here are three titles that you can find in your local video shop that make work seem funny:

1. Big (US '88)
2. Toys (US '92)
3. The Simpsons (particularly Simpson and Delilah)

You'll be surprised at what you learn when you interpret these films as examinations of the place of man at work.

L is also for...

Learning and Teaching

The shy man will not learn;
the impatient man should not teach.
Ask and learn.

Hillel the Elder

Cultivate those who can teach you.

Baltasar Gracian

To teach is to learn twice.

Joseph Joubert

Where are the experts in your organization?

Do they spend enough of their time teaching others how to do what they do so expertly? Or do they use their expertise to stand out from the crowd and protect their own patch?

Are all your people appraised on their teaching skills?

The Ultimate Motivational Empowerment question: Could you show me how to do that?[37]

Learning should be a crucial, hot area of your business – people should be excited to learn. There's too much happening to think that you know enough already.

There is, I'm sure, a wealth of knowledge in your company which is barely realised.

And I don't just mean **skills**

- although I don't know why you should spend money on external customer care training when everybody knows that the best example of excellent service in your company is Hassan over in security.

---

[37] I once saw the CEO of Ford prove that he could change the oil on a Taurus by doing it, which impressed me, the rest of the television viewers and, I imagine, his staff.

...and Training

I also mean **attitudes**.

A highly successful manager once talked to me about a colleague of his.

- 'I've been in this company as long as Nick, and I've gone further. But there's one thing that bothers me: I wish I could be as funny as him. How do you think he does it?'

My suggestion that he should find out from Nick (who presumably was better placed to tell him than I was) was greeted with horror. You might have thought I was asking him to proposition Nick in the toilets.

'Funniness'. That's an example of an attitude available in one employee that might be valuable for the whole company to have. It's an example of where they might have got it, and of why they didn't.

But let's go back to skills.

Sending your people on training courses – even if you send your people on more courses per head than all your competitors put together – isn't enough unless those courses are excellent. And I mean the best – stimulating, stretching, inspirational. I'm talking Robin Williams in *Dead Poets Society* (US '89) rather than Gradgrind in *Hard Times*. Some training out there today is as deadly dull as the business it tries to improve and some of the buying-in of these services is just as half-hearted and formulaic. This is counterproductive for all concerned – a waste of your people's time and your money.

You want your people to have experienced change, not gained a certificate for turning up.

L is also for...

Liberation
Or 'These Little Things'

You should be asking:

- 'What would make your life at work better?'

And don't be surprised at the answers.

You will find from the feedback that you are seeking and encouraging – formally and informally, on paper and face to face – that ridiculously small changes would make those improvements.

There you are building The Strategy and there they are fed up about the lack of pencil-sharpeners.

One man I know craved the opportunity just to turn his desk at an angle of 90 degrees so that it faced the door and not the wall. He wanted to see people and be seen – he wanted to be involved. But he didn't feel powerful enough to make that simple change.

Another woman complained to me recently that she would love to be able to put her feet up on her desk:

- 'What!' I roared, They pay you all that money and they won't even let you put your feet up?'

  'It's not that,' she replied, 'It's the fact that they won't let me wear trousers...'.

L is also for...

Listening

From listening comes wisdom; from speaking comes repentance.

Italian proverb

Suffer fools gladly. They may be right.

Holbrook Jackson

Listening is one of the key skills involved in building trust and, because we don't do it well enough, it is another one of the main reasons that we

a) fail to show ourselves to be trustworthy, and

b) fail to build trusting relationships.

And a lack of trusting relationships is a dead-sure prerequisite for a fun-free workplace. Just ask around.

I'm not talking here about the 'aha, uhuh, mmm' noises that they teach you on those listening skills courses to prove that you're still awake and attentive. I'm talking about listening for the messages carried beneath the words, or in the tone of voice and the pauses and the emphasis and the body language, or even in what is not said. I'm talking about listening to understand; and that means seeing the other person's point of view not just as if through their eyes but also through their heart and mind.

Listening means shutting up – shutting up our thoughts and preconceptions as much as our mouths. But what really happens?[38]

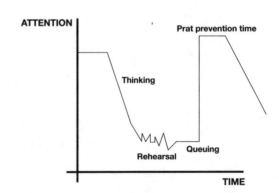

HOW TO MAKE WORK FUN!

Further Listening

We do listen for a short period of time but soon we start to think about what is being said. And thought is a private occupation. Soon, we begin to rehearse alternative responses – such activity makes it difficult for us to concentrate. Having decided on our chosen response, we queue – we simply wait for the other party to stop talking. At last, as soon as we sense that we may have an opportunity to speak, we concentrate entirely on the other person. But why? To make sure that our response is in some way relevant to what is currently being talked about: the moments that we check that we are not about to make a prat of ourselves.

That's why conversations seem such hard work: we're doing all this work when we should be doing nothing. We're as egotistical as self-obsessed actors; we don't want to let anybody else's lines intrude. We're too busy preparing for our own performance – and, hey everybody, get ready – that performance may only be one more sentence away.

There are skills to learn that improve our ability to shut up and concentrate on what people are trying to say to us. But what is really needed is a basic shift in attitude to our place in the world: that we must genuinely understand before we worry about being understood.

[38]My thanks to Darrel Poulos of Poulos & Partners.

A Litmus

Does your organ

Human beings draw close to
but habits and c

C

Imagine this...

Your board meeting is just ending. Someone tells a joke — and I mean a really good one. Everybody — everybody — is laughing, hooting, crying, falling off their chairs. Look! Even the sides of the Finance Director's face are moving! As you begin to gasp for breath and hold your sides, you are thinking that this could possibly be the funniest joke that you have ever heard in your life. Wow! It actually feels good to be here

t for Fun

need this book?

nother by their very nature,
keep them apart.
is.

And then...

A client walks in.

What happens?

What's the predominant emotion in the room?

Shame.

'Sorry.'

Recognize that emotion? Ah yes.

Feels like school, eh?

There are two things you can do to make things better:

1. Get clients that don't mind you laughing.

2. Use this book. You've made a stain on the litmus paper.

is for

Meetings

Moods

More! Meetings

Motivation

M is for...

Meetings

A meeting is a gathering of people seeking refuge from the dreariness of labour and the loneliness of thought.

Anonymous

So there are meetings, and meetings about meetings, and meetings to plan reports, and meetings to review the status of reports. And what these meetings are about is people just trying to figure out what they are doing.

Paul Strassman, former Vice President, Xerox Corp.

Some good places for a meeting:

- Anywhere standing up at 6 p.m. on a Friday
- In the car park
- In the park
- At the zoo
- At your home
- Under the biggest clock in town
- In the gym.

Bloody Meetings!

Some questions being asked silently in meetings:

- Do I need to be here?
- How can I cover up what I haven't done?
- Is it true what they say about public shamings being more painful than private ones?
- Will I be involved?
- How long will it take before X shouts everybody else down?
- Why are we just reading these reports out to each other?

Some good questions to ask, and suggestions on the time spent answering each:

- What are we doing?   (10%)
- What has that to do with the price of fish?[39]   (30%)
- What can we do next?   (55%)
- What have we done?   (5%)

Don't bother with minutes, always bother with action points.

[39] That is, does it accord with our mission, vision, aim, sense of being? Does it look to the long term?

The Challenge Page!

THE CHALLENGE

Pick the most boring financially-based meeting next week. Rename it 'The Exorcist' or 'Indiana Jones and the Temple of Doom' or 'Don Giovanni' and rename the attendees accordingly. Turn the challenges that you have met to debate into plot lines, scary twists and climaxes. You could even bring some props.

THE COP-OUT

Your top excuses for not daring to do it:

- The work will not stand this sort of ribaldry.
- The participants may not be able to take themselves or each other seriously.
- All those numbers will collapse under the weight of lightness.
- Seeing important tasks from a new perspective may inspire creative solutions.

Remember — 41%![40]

You don't have much time.

Let me know how it goes!

[40]See p. 4.

M is also for...

Moods

Can there be misery...[he yawns]...loftier than mine?

Hamm, *Endgame*, Samuel Beckett

Moods come and go

They can be a good thing (see D is for Dissatisfaction); but here I address the problem of Plain Old Grumpy-Drawers.

It helps to realize that you create all your moods through what you choose to focus on, the way you interpret events and the way you use your body.[41] The usual immediate reaction to this realization – that is, to pin the blame for your moods on to someone or something else – is itself all part of the process of projecting meaning onto what you choose to see. So is the justification that nobody feels those moods as strongly as you do.

The consolation from this realization is that you can change your moods by changing what you focus on, the way you interpret events and the way you use your body. And you should work to change your bad moods – moody people are the victims of self-inflicted patterns of behaviour and life is challenging enough without putting yourself through that.

Some solutions to moodiness

With *others*:

1. Tell people that you think that you are moody – are you right?

2. Listen to feedback – how does the mood manifest itself and what does it cost (i.e. how does it make others feel and what isn't achieved because of it)?

3. Ask for help and absolve them of responsibility. Let them know that you are not going to be annoyed or hold it against them in the future.

4. Brainstorm solutions – devise code words or panic buttons that you all can press when the mood comes on, for example 'Mark, the Professor is back!'

5. Keep to their action plan and your promises.

---

[41]See W is for When it all gets too much.

...and Moods

By *yourself*:

1. A three step approach:

   (a) Become aware of what you think, feel and do when you are in a mood.

   (b) Become aware of what you think, feel and do just before you get into a mood.

   (c) Take action to interrupt the pattern of thoughts and feelings at (b) rather than (a).

2. Go for a walk.

3. Throw yourself into a conversation about an unrelated topic.

4. Listen to a favourite piece of music or reach into your Fun Tool Kit.

5. Make a strange noise. (I do. Colleagues of mine will now realize what I've been up to. Whenever I feel embarrassment coming on – for me a disabling mood caused by feeling guilty about past cock-ups – I launch myself into a series of vocal sounds which are a cross between humming and coughing. It breaks the pattern that would otherwise encourage the mood to develop. It works.)

What to do about other people's moods is something else. Working with Mr Sulk and Ms Sad all the time is no fun. It takes guts to explain to someone that they are dragging you down with them into the Slough of Despond (in Essex, just off the M25, karaoke on Friday nights).

It is even more difficult to want to help rather than punish them. But you have to accept that we bring more of ourselves to work than just our technical ability and that what work should be about is trying to get our collective selves to move towards the same business objective. This includes our emotions. Too many bad moods do not make a liberating environment.

Tackle the problem by adapting the kinds of analysis listed under the 'with others' solutions to moodiness above.

Then introduce 'Moods and how we deal with them' into the appraisal system.

M is also for...

More! Meetings

In times of stress or adversity, call More! meetings. All participants should bring one example of something that's going well in the team, project or organization.

Or start every meeting like that. Agenda?

> Minutes of the last meeting
>
> Apologies
>
> More!
>
> etc.

Then gradually remove 'Minutes of the last meeting' and 'Apologies'.

it.

M is also for...

Motivation

The carrot and stick approach to extracting the best out of your people is outdated. The world of work has changed. The carrots are becoming less crunchy. The stick is less pointy. And you can't get a donkey on a roller-coaster.

We are right to suppose that the best way to motivate someone is to appeal to what is important to them. We are wrong to decide, on behalf of the people we are trying to motivate, what those things are. It's better, if more difficult, to ask. We need to find out what those motivations are and then to separate them into the extrinsic and the intrinsic. For example:

extrinsic motivations

- leadership or management communications
- work relationships
- salary
- bonus structure
- promotion opportunities
- physical environment
- access to information and systems
- job specifications
- holidays

intrinsic motivations

- values
- self-esteem
- skills deployment and development

More Motivation

- ethical and spiritual considerations.

Give yourself a couple of hours and have an informal conversation guided by the following questions:

1. Just a minute. Hang on. Now, where's my pen? Ahah! Right. Sorry.

2. Which of the extrinsic motivations could work better for you? How? Why? What do you want to feel by improving that extrinsic motivation?

3. Which of the intrinsic motivations concern you most at work? Which do you feel are being offended, subdued or ignored?

4. How do you identify with your work?

5. What things are you proud of in your life, what qualities do you demonstrate well outside work which you feel could be better exploited here? How could we let that happen?

6. How do you compare what's happened to you in your personal life (e.g. examples of recognition, reward from family members, etc.) with similar experiences at work? How could we make one feel more like the other?

Persevere. There'll be many blank stares and quizzical silences but I'm sure there were too when Newton was first feeling his way towards the Theory of Gravity.

If you don't learn anything and it doesn't give you ideas on how to make changes in the way work is done in your company, then I'm wrong and I'm sorry, or you're not listening and I'm sorry.

With questions like these – and I'm not going to pretend that these are exactly the right ones – we are moving towards a system that will help people to understand themselves, to understand what it is that makes them do what they do and not do what they should do. Furthermore, they might tell us how those new discoveries can be applied to the work that we do, how that work might be done better, or whether the person you are talking to might be better suited to a different job.

Fresh Motivation

We all need to know that we are not victims of chance or the mortgage. We need a sense that there may be certain environments that encourage us, certain triggers that motivate us, certain skills and styles that we need with which we can excel. Especially we need to know that these can be designed, or redesigned, if it results in new levels of personal and professional performance.

This has not been offered as a new theory of motivation – the subject is too complex to cover in a short section. But I think that motivation questions like these will achieve two benefits:

1. They will feed that fascination for people without which management must be a dry and sterile affair.[42]

2. People like to be listened to. I've heard many people say that they don't work as well as they could because the pay is bad or because the office is too hot. But mostly I hear people say that they are dissatisfied with their company because they feel nobody cares about them.

Two Things I Saw on Holiday (v

The point being that if you open your eyes you can see

1. Employee photographs
– getting a look at everybody who works here

At a famous chain of American supermarkets, every employee has their photograph pinned up on the 'we are here to help you' board in the lobby – and then they sign their name underneath. This happens whether you work on the checkout, where you'll meet many customers, or in the warehouse, where you won't.

Now I have no idea if this is one of the main reasons that this chain of supermarkets is growing faster than many of its competitors. I do know that people in photographs tend to smile and a wall full of smiling people (they are photographed doing their jobs, by the way; no startled rabbit passport shots) strikes me as a good first impression of the store.

It also makes me think of client relationships. Who is your main contact at your supplier company? Yes, it's Terry the Project Manager. And just how 'main' is that contact? Who do you talk to in the course of that project? Terry a lot, of course, but also Bob and Jenny (Terry's team mates) and Andy and Rebecca (who work in the office next door) and also Stephanie (whoever she is) when they're all out at lunch spending your money. And every single time you contact your supplier you speak to Natalie the switchboard operator. Come to think of it, in frequency terms, you probably speak to all those other people more often than you speak to Terry.

---

[43]Single photos of (smile on) 'Your Customer Service representative' (smile off) do not count. Nor do those ridiculous group portraits of the Board that you sometimes find in annual reports. I always think those photos make them look like models on the front of a knitting pattern.

really looking) **That Looked Like Fun**

aving fun at work. Or maybe people are different in America.

Wouldn't it be good to put some faces to those voices?

In 1988, researchers at Ohio State University played to their subjects audio tapes of various people disclaiming their part in a crime. In addition, some subjects were shown photographs of people and told that they were of some of the speakers. The subjects were then told that half of the people to whom they were listening were, in fact, entirely truthful and innocent – the others were involved in the crime and were lying. In a significantly high majority of cases, subjects chose the voices of those whose photographs they had been shown as belonging to the innocent parties. In most cases, they chose to disbelieve those voices that remained 'anonymous'.

This experiment implies that you are more likely to believe Stephanie or Andy when they tell you why Terry hasn't got in yet at 11 a.m. if you have seen them. I would also think it implies that you are more likely to be able to chat freely with them, share a joke with them, confide in them and generally increase the depth and breadth of your supplier relationship beyond just poor old Terry, if you know what they look like. In other words, you are able to make all those human transactions that take the place of contacting Terry a little more fun.

I have never seen a 'meet the (whole) team' photo gallery at the back of any project plan. I have seen very few employee photo boards in the lobby of companies, even fewer that engage rather than frighten me.

I mustn't be looking hard enough. Please put me right and let me know.[43]

(Turn page for the second thing I saw.)

Two Things I Saw on Holiday (w

The point being that if you open your eyes you can see p

2. Ellen
— A Big Casino — Las Vegas — 2.8.94

OK, so you can't really see a conversation, but the way that Ellen served us our breakfast seemed to me to be the epitome of excellent service.

Here was a waitress who was in the middle of a shift during which (I later found out) she would serve over 500 guests. And yet the effortless way in which she greeted us, smiled, commiserated with my father-in-law who was having trouble with his hearing aid, played mock-hurt when we teased her for forgetting a side order and, later, waved us off into the day, suggested three things to me:

[44]A small Scottish bird.

HOW TO MAKE WORK FUN!

(really looking) **That Looked Like Fun**

ing fun at work. Or maybe people are different in America.

1. That you are never going to have fun at work if all you can concentrate on are the negatives, even though you may possess enough negatives for everybody.

2. That your customers don't really give a flying hoot[44] about your troubles, except in the context of how well you are battling with them.

3. That we create our own environments. If you decide to be upbeat, positive, happy, light, you will create for yourself a job that offers its own rewards. If you decide to be miserable, angry, bitter, dark, you will create that environment for yourself and your colleagues around you.

In Ellen's words:

'If I decide to be happy, it makes my job easier for me. If I come in miserable, exactly the same work seems harder'.

is for

Needs

N is for...

Needs

Why do people go to work at all? They need money, but that isn't the sole reason why they work. Productive work satisfies a whole host of requirements, of which only one is money. This is as true for the six-figure salary executive as it is for the low-wage employee. The money may be vital, but it is not the reason why they stay or go, perform or fail.

This is seen in the behaviour of some of our most talented executives, or so I read. They create empires, sell-up to make personal fortunes, rest and relax for a year or so, and then become restless and start all over again. It isn't greed. It's a desire to make something more of themselves.

The psychologists and sociologists give us similar suggestions. Schulz describes community in terms of fulfilling powerful self-needs – affection, inclusion, respect, relationships, love (and, ironically enough, bearing in mind the humbug managers of yesterday), our need to control things. Similarly, we can only move up Maslow's hierarchy to produce a sense of worth and esteem for the self by moving into community with others.

Rather more beautifully, A.M. Hocart suggests that society organizes itself around a life-giving myth – a ritual which is supposed to supply hope, opportunity and growth. The myth offers the hope of a successful life (over the elements, over enemies, over poverty, and so on). Our organizations, therefore, give us the opportunity to generate meaning in life – a sense that we are producing, with others who are like us, something greater than ourselves.

Continued Needs?

Like widgets and things

As C.W. Metcalf and Roma Felible, the noted American humourists and consultants, summarize in their book *Lighten Up* (Addison-Wesley, 1992):

> Some theorise that the need for community is learned; others believe it's genetic, a survival mechanism woven into our DNA. Clearly, as a species, people were clumsier, slower, and less well armed than a lot of other carnivores. Through a combination of luck, flexibility, intelligence (which was not necessarily greater than that of dolphins), and, most important, teamwork and cooperation, they survived and thrived...Although Hollywood tells us otherwise, if it were possible to pit a muscle man like Arnold Schwarzenegger against a tiger, the tiger would win. But allow a group of people – even total nerds – to hunt, or merely build a housing development in the habitat of the beast, and eventually the human tribe will triumph.

Is your tribe flourishing? Or are the tigers picking off a set of isolated and lonely individuals?

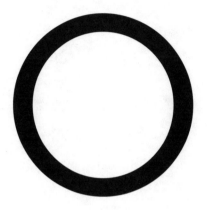

is for

Of Mice and Men

O is for...

Of Mice and Men

I am pleased to include a short extract from the recently discovered first draft of that great American novel *Of Mice and Men* by John Steinbeck:

'Tell me how it's gonna be, George. About the rabbits, and such'.

'Well, Lenny, we gonna get a little place...', said George.

'And,' interrupted Lenny eagerly, 'we will work together in teams, yes we will, sir. And our organizations will sing the joy of co-operation (because they are, after all, corporations)...'.

'Yes Lenny...'.

'...and nobody will want to get over his bad experiences at boarding school by wanting to make work a punishment for not marrying into a rich family...'.

'Yes Lenny...'.

'...and our leaders will be charismatic, human, communicating, emotional human beings, and we will all know that labour without joy is base, and we will all live off the fat of the land...

'Oh shut it, you **soppy, liberal, nursery school, right-brained, nonsense, left-wing time-waster, my people won't have fun, they'll have a job!!!!'**

And George pulled the trigger, and Lenny slumped forward into the alfalfa patch.

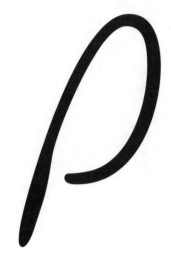

is for

Passion

Performance Appraisals

Permission

Proof

P is for...

Passion

There are a growing number of people who are becoming passionate about their work and the meaning it has for them.

They describe passion as having two useful facets. There is the passion of love and desire – go for it, strive for what you believe in, for what you love. But there is also the passion that shows itself as anger, or even outrage, when they feel that they are being deprived of what's important to them.

P is also for...

Performance Appraisals

You want your people to work harder, faster, smarter? Fine, but they might have some suggestions as to how you can improve. Only humbug managers say, 'My seniority means that I know better than you'. Smart managers are too scared to miss anything that might make things better. They also acknowledge that others may know better, or have valuable insights from having actually done the work.

Implement more informal, and better formal, appraisals. Allow two-way appraisals – let both participants have a form and appraise each other.

Some companies are doing 360 degree appraisals where the subject is appraised by:

1. A person above them
2. A person below them
3. A peer
4. A customer
5. A supplier.

Undertake appraisals on neutral ground. Do them regularly (every two to six months or after key events) to send the messages of continuity, action and listening. Keep it in terms of people getting better or worse, increasing or decreasing, rather than mechanical rankings or marking. Ensure that absolute honesty and openness are the first (the only?) two rules of this interaction.

Make sure the appraisals acknowledge the fundamental truth that all life is subjective and that business, because it is run by people, is more psychological than logical. You should be looking at whether your people are liked, whether customers enjoy their company, how well they seem to be doing, how creative they feel... .

How do we decide whether or not to stay at the party?

Performance Appraisals Plus

We don't calibrate the dimensions of the room. We get a feel for the atmosphere. And that's how it should be with our people. Any old fool can be found to do the work,[45] what matters is whether they are good to be with for 41% of our lives.[46]

Here's a list of other items the appraisal form could include:

- Short- and long-term objectives and the training needs they imply.
- What am I like at work (what's my meaning)?
- What obstacles am I finding here?
- How am I improving?
- What am I learning?
- Reasons I've had for feeling fear or guilt at work.
- Best thing that happened to me/I did at home during the last period.
- Best thing that happened to me/I did at work during the last period.

And every time, just in case you are sitting on the star entrepreneur of tomorrow, include a wider corporate angle. Ask them to complete this sentence:

> If this organization were to start from scratch tomorrow and I were in charge, I would change...

[45] I'm exaggerating for poetic effect, but you understand my point.
[46] See p. 4.

1. Go for a walk in the park or visit an art gallery. Or both.

2. See how many film titles/book titles you can say in a meeting without being noticed (a good game to play with a friend).

3. Have files marked 'dull', 'duller', 'unspeakably dull'; 'unfortunately urgent', etc.

4. Get screen savers for your PCs – if you already have them, hold a screen saver creation competition.

5. Have a legends box – objects that make you remember key moments – or a Polaroid board to do the same.

6. Encourage people to grow a small plant on their desk.

7. Put a few armchairs into a reading and chatting and relaxing area.

Things

introduce some life into work:

8. Arrange a Job Intelligence Day with neighbouring companies — of the same industry if you'd prefer, but more interestingly of other industries — so that your people can go out and benchmark. Finding out how the local cemetery stonemason deals with customers or measures quality might give you an interesting perspective on how you carry out the same kind of operation in your marketing department

9. Make a resolution not to become suspicious when you hear people laughing.

10. Beg, steal or borrow the budget to bring in someone to teach your team how to juggle. Please do this. Think: a three-hour workshop, spread over a week. Three hours? A couple of hundred pounds (if that)? For a new skill and a great stress reducer and an important team builder? Come on. It really doesn't get any easier than this.

    I'm still a lousy juggler, but it makes me laugh every time I try, and it makes me wonder at those who can.

P is also for...

Permission

It is easier to beg forgiveness than to ask permission.
Jesuit principle

At school, we used to ask permission to leave the class to visit the toilet. This device was designed to teach the child respect for its elders and to put a restraint on children's notoriously weak self-discipline. Because sometimes when we are young we don't really go to the toilet; we sneak off and hide behind the bicycle sheds.

Whatever your views on the current state of education, business shouldn't be vying with schools to finish off lessons in manners and discipline. If you have people in your organization who want to sneak off and hide behind the bicycle sheds, then they probably feel so constricted and weak that they still want to rebel against authority. Let them grow up and be who they are. Treating them like children by requesting them to ask permission to be allowed to do things is not going to make things any better.

The only rule in this area is that of courtesy – it's better to know if a team member is going to be on holiday next month, or if he or she is going to take a long lunch break. Utilize a calendar and coloured tags and let them get on with it.

Asking permission promotes distrust, inhibits action and teaches guilt.

P is also for...

Proof

I'm not going to give you any. There are studies that make a link between contentment, involvement and productivity, but this isn't the place for them. You'll be wanting a definition of fun next.

If you don't **feel** that work should be fun, if you don't have a **sense** that your organization would be a better place if it could apply some of the ideas in this book, you certainly won't be convinced by a few numbers on a graph.

This book isn't for you. Take it back to the shop and ask them to refund your money in full. Or better still, bring it round to my house and I'll refund your money ten-fold and pay your travel expenses. It'll be worth it. I've always wanted to meet a humourless bastard like you.

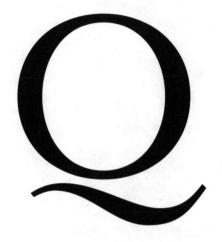

is for

Questions

Quotations

Q is for...

Questions

Some men see things as they are, and say 'Why?'
I dream of things that never were, and say, 'Why not?'

George Bernard Shaw

The questions we ask about any situation determine:

1. Our perspective and view on the situation.

2. The resources of energy and imagination we apply to the situation.

3. Ultimately, the result.

Ask questions that demand positive responses or action and that support a 'can-do' culture.

When asking after somebody's work, don't ask:

'How is it going?'

but ask:

'Can I see what you've done so far?'

or

'Will you take me through what you have been doing so that I can understand?'

When faced with a problem, don't say:

'It's OK; I'll deal with it!'

but ask:

'What would you do to fix this?'

or

'If I'd taken a drug that allowed me only to see the positive aspects of this problem, what would I see?'

or

'How can we learn from this problem?'

Questions have the power to affect our beliefs and what we think is possible or impossible. The language we use in response to those questions is a key part of this process towards effective learning and vigorous action.[47]

[47]See L is for Language.

Q is also for...

Quotations

I love them, because it is a joy to find thoughts one might have, beautifully expressed with much authority by someone recognizably wiser than oneself.

Marlene Dietrich, *Marlene Dietrich's ABC*

Include a quotation in every document you send out – every memo, every proposal, every invoice.[48]

It stretches the sender's imagination, it entertains the receiver, it puts business into perspective, it's fun.

And besides, Shakespeare knew more about ambition than Sir John Harvey-Jones. And Groucho Marx had a thicker moustache than Sir John Harvey-Jones, and was funnier.

---

[48]'Payable within 30 days of receipt' does not count.

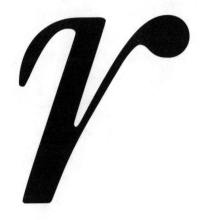

is for

Ranting

Recruitment

R is for...

Ranting

ENOUGH

OFTHEFARCETHATBUSINESSISTHERETODIVIDETASKSANDALLOCA
TESEPARATERESOURCESENOUGHOFTHEFARCETHATBUSINESSIST
HERETOMEASURETHINGSOBJECTIVELYTHEONLYTRUEBUSINESSI
SINTERACTIONORINTERCONNECTIVITYPARTICIPATIONISTHENEWC
ORECOMPETENCEGETTINGONISTHENEWSCIENCEGODDAMMITPO
WERLEADSTOCONTROLWHICHLEADSTOSELFISHNESSANDPOSSE
SSIVENESSANDDEFENSIVENESSANDFEAR(THEEXACTOPPPOSITES
OFTHELOVEANDCHANGEANDCOMMITMENTTOSERVICETHATWEA
RESUPPOSEDTONEEDTOSURVIVE!!!)THISISANUGLYBEHAVIOURAL
TRUTHANDASHUMANBEINGSWESHOULDACCEPTTHATWEHAVETH
ISPOTENTIALFORDOINGTHEWRONGTHINGREGULARLYLISTENTO
METHEBESTWECANDOISPLACEOURSELVESINSTRUCTURESTHATD
ONOTENCOURAGESUCHDISSOLUTIONBUTASLONGASOURORGANI
ZATIONSDIVIDEANDSEPARATEANDPOWERREMAINSTHECHIEFRE
WARDANDOBJECTIVEOFOURPEOPLETHENWE'LLBELOCKEDINTOT
HELOOPWHATAWASTEHELLSBELLSTHECOMPANIESTHATNURTUR
EUSINTHEFUTUREWILLBETHOSETHATREWARDUSWITHASENSEOF
ACHIEVEMENTTHROUGHSERVICETOOTHERSRATHERTHANDOMIN
IONOVEROTHERSIKNOWIKNOWIKNOWI'MNOTKIDDINGMYSELFTH
ATFORMANYTHEFUNOFWORKWILLREMAININTHEVERYPOWERAN
DPOLITICSTHATDRAGSUSDOWNIJUSTWISHTHEY'DLAUGHATTHEM
SELVESABITMORETHOSEINPOWERARERIDICULOUSNOTBECAUSE
OFWHOTHEYAREBUTBECAUSETHEYARESOVISIBLEWEGETTOWATC
HTHEMALLTHETIMETHEBESTLEADERSHAVEADISARMINGABILITYT
OLAUGHATTHEMSELVES

This rant was brought to you by The Rant Organization.

Ranting On

Rants are fun because they allow us to exaggerate and provoke, and the sheer physical and emotional exercise that ranting entails provides a release of tension. You can say what you feel at the moment without anybody holding you to it later. And, besides, when you get going, sometimes good sense emerges with all the rest.

If you rant enough, you'll have an outlet for anger and frustration and perceived impotence, before they turn into personal nightmares, where dark shadows recreate themselves and feed themselves on our fears. These nightmares cloud our judgement and obscure our perception of what is truth. Then the stress and worry kills us whilst we are young.

Hold it in all you like; it will not go away until you let it out.

Tibetan saying

R is also for...

Recruitment

Become totally involved in it

Recruitment is a negotiation – an interaction between buyer and seller. Take every interview as an opportunity to promote your skills in **Influencing** by selling the positive values and thrilling uniqueness of your organization. Even if you can't give the candidate the job, you should be aiming to send him or her off:

1. Handing in an application form to have another attempt even as they leave.

2. Envious of your colleagues in being lucky enough to work there.

3. Spreading the word about how good your place is.

Who should be doing the interviewing?

Three people:

1. Somebody very senior.

2. Someone who will be working alongside the lucky candidate.

3. The person who is leaving.

All three should be honest. Tell the candidates what your weaknesses are; tell them why six different people have filled this position in a single year, and what you are doing to fix the attrition. If you don't like the candidate, tell them why – help them improve. If they had a huge bogey hanging from their nose, they'll need to know before their next interview.

Further Recruitment

And for whom should you be looking?

Rule Number One in personnel departments around the world: 'Thou shalt not consider for employment any individual who has so much as a nanosecond's gap in their resume between birth and the present moment'. But I'll tell you who I want to hire. I want to hire that young woman who went off to the Massachusetts Institute of Technology...to get a degree in computer science; who had a 3.8 out of 4 average mid-way through her sophomore year and who, mid-way through that sophomore year, decided that the Massachusetts Institute of Technology was one of the dullest institutions ever created by God on His Earth. And so she took off. She took off around the world for two years. We don't have a clue as to what the hell she did: she may have worked for Mother Teresa; she may have been a chainsaw murderer. We don't know. But what we do know, when we see her, is that at least at one point in this human being's life she did something slightly out of the ordinary, and maybe, just maybe, if we are lucky, she may do something out of the ordinary for us.

Tom Peters, *Crazy Ways for Crazy Days*, BBC TV

Ask yourself

not:

- 'Will they fit the job?'

but:

- 'What's new or different about this person?'
- 'How will they add to my team?'
- 'What new, improved role can I create around their specific talents?'

If you only have square holes to fill then you are only ever going to be able to hire square pegs.

And finally, what's the best possible atmosphere or mood in which to conduct an interview?

Curiosity!

is for

Sad Song

Silly

Space

Space (again)

Spies

Stop

Stress

S is for...

Sad Song

The saddest song I ever hear:

> *'Well, that's OK for you...'*

as in 'Well that's OK for you...

- you're a consultant'
- you work for another company'
- you work for yourself'
- you're more senior than I am'
- you're more junior than I am'
- you have a different shoe size'
- it could never happen here'.

Somebody, somewhere owns the royalties to this song and they are growing richer and richer every time we sing it.

The Ten Point Hip, Thigh

Discovering th

1. Make fun of yourself

You have unlimited material to work with.

2. Learn to relax

There are a hundred techniques available to cultivate a relaxed state of mind and body. I'm not going to patronize you by repeating them here — besides, other writers need their royalties. If you really don't know, find out, because stress is probably killing you. You probably have many friends, acquaintances and colleagues who are better at applying stress management techniques than you — you should ask them. Only recently, for goodness' sake, my mother-in-law told me of a stress-reducing exercise that I'd never heard of. In this day and age you have no excuse not to be able to relax through means other than the drinks cabinet. The only inhibitor to your personal well-being is your attitude — an attitude that probably tells you that you are too busy not to be stressed. Don't listen: it's lying to you.

3. Tease people

It often helps others to see themselves from another perspective, so especially tease people who don't follow point one above.

Teasing is a great deflator and much needed in work, a place that brings out our worst propensity for self-importance.

Teasing is a good thing:

- as long as it shows care not pride.
- as long as it is inclusive not exclusive.
- as long as it diffuses tension and seeks solutions.

Tummy Fun Programme

UN Inside You

4. Look for the funny side of events

Stop trying to understand life, it's not your job. Instead, look for patterns, repetitions, similarities, myths in life – they will show you that under the sun there is nothing new and that therefore you are unlikely to be responsible for it. One of the key skills of the funny person is recognizing those patterns and making the connections – Yes, it's just like that, isn't it? You mean that's happened to you too?

This is why professional comedians mock our futile attempts to make sense of the world.

You can't have everything. Where would you put it?

Steven Wright

5. Be fascinated by people [49]

If you're not fascinated you can't understand and if you can't understand then you can't learn.

Similarly, fascination precludes judgement. The only one who understands people entirely is Ol' Grandaddy Aloft, which is probably why he undertakes all the judging on The Big P45 Day (I know a few people who live as if they are in training for this job, but, as far as I know, the position is taken). Absolved from this weighty responsibility, we can concentrate on the variety, complexity and possibility in human behaviour and our attempts to perform – and do so with lots of curiosity and a minimum of anger.

---

[49]This fascination should extend to your own behaviour: 'Why *do* I keep doing that?'.

6. Know what you believe in

It helps you stop bitching about what others believe in — a sure sign that you have never really sorted out what's important to you.

7. Exercise your humour muscle

- Read comics.
- Listen to comics.
- Write down your best fun experiences — what happened, how it felt, how it might be possible to repeat the feeling.

8. Seek happiness

Write a 'Reasons to be Cheerful' list .[50]

---

[50] See H is for Happiness.
[51] I've got a horrible feeling you wanted things to be more complicated than this.

Tummy Fun Programme

FUN inside you

9. Smile

(a) Smiling moves the muscles in your face which encourages more blood to carry oxygen to your brain and this releases encephalins and endorphins from your brain stem. Encephalins and endorphins are what help dull the pain when you chop your finger off, but if you aren't injured, they just make you feel good.

Wow!

This drug is free and it is good for you. You don't have to hang around in public parks for your dealer to turn up. It doesn't rot your nasal cavities. It's the only non-prescription drug apart from caffeine that you can use at work. You can drive under its influence. Responsible for operating heavy machinery? Go ahead!

Just don't tell the government I told you about it.

(b) Smiling is a pleasant thing to look at and it tends to have a pleasant effect on the people around you.[51] They may well smile back, and that will make you feel good too. If you are not careful here, you may create a positive spiral.

10. Always round off lists to satisfyingly whole numbers

S is also for...

Silly

Here's a sad fact.

Back in medieval times, when we all used to speak Old English, we had a word

ge-saelig

which meant 'completely happy; blessed'. We used to greet each other in our muddy streets, and say:

'Ge-saelig'

or in Modern English

'Go: be happy today.' [52]

From *ge-saelig* we derive *silly*. Silly used to have all that potential for happiness, individuality, being in a blessed state. But then the humbuggers stamped that happiness out straight away. We have completely lost the potential for positive fun through silliness. How do you know when two people are relaxed and getting on? They tease each other. They make silly references at strange times. It is that state – relaxed, open, confident – that you want to instil in your team, and if silly behaviour is the natural byproduct, then you should be

Celebrating!

that you've built such a closely-knit team.

Don't forget to be silly from time to time. It won't demean either you or the work – both are big enough to stand it. And being silly is a sign to everyone else that you are still alive. Too much gravity gets you

down.

---

[52]The Americans, naturally vivacious and vivaciously natural, still retain 'Have a nice day!' but it's just not the same.

S is also for...

Space

Who first invented Work – and tied the free
And holy-day rejoicing spirit down
To the ever-haunting importunity
Of business, in the green fields, and the town –
To plough – loom – anvil – spade – and, oh, most sad,
To this dry drudgery of the desk's dead wood?

Charles Lamb

1. Give yourself some space

(a) in the office

The office of the near future will be a place where you won't feel guilty about closing your eyes, because people will know that you are thinking or imagining or creating. Or even better, they'll know that you are taking a nap and they won't care!

(b) out of the office

When I went independent, one of the main dreams I had was that self-employment would allow me to go shopping during the day. Imagine! Such banality! Such freedom. It has.

I work in an environment that trusts me to come back, to do the job whenever I deem fit. Going shopping isn't a liberty or a theft of time or a threat to the company discipline. Who cares?

(c) way out of the office

Take all of your holiday allowance. Relentless pressure kills. Absolutely.

2. Give your team some space

Leave the team to have space and enjoy it. Where did I hear that best practice in management in the 1990s would be measured by the ability to move out of the way?

S is also for...

Space (again)

The Create-Your-Own-Best-Space Workshop

Step 1

Using coloured pens, cut-outs from magazines, etc., create a collage that represents your ideal working space.

Step 2

Now having created that vision, how can you recreate it in your environment? Maybe you can't have a 1000 sq. ft circular office on top of a skyscraper, but how could you mimic one? Could you introduce mirrors to give a sense of space? What objects would you have around? If you hung your skis above your desk would it be a constant reminder of you at your most exhilarated and free? How would you light your space? What would you sit on? What 'Symbols of Me'[53] would you bring in to reflect and stimulate your expression and independence?

Step 3

Take the collage to your boss and ask why your space can't be like that. If the answer is 'Go ahead, here's £100 towards the cost', great. If it's 'we can't – what would I do if everyone came to me with these crazy demands', then give me a call for some free career advice...

Let me tell you a story about a company I know where the employees became blocked. They didn't enjoy the work much any more. There wasn't a great deal of work about (maybe the two were connected). They were struggling with new ideas. They were struggling with relationships. They needed a boost, a stimulant. So they thought, 'well what can we actually do to change how we feel? We want more customers – that would make us feel better – but we can't just wave a wand to find them. We can paint the office though – hey, we've got the time!'

[53] See B is for Banalities.

Space (again)
Again

So they all came to work, dressed for some real work – in overalls and boiler suits. They transferred all telephone calls to an answering service. They carried everything out into the car park. They went back into the empty shell of their old office and they designed and painted their new office. That was Friday.

On the Monday they went shopping. They bought toys, posters, plants, strange carpet tiles. They bought holders that allowed them to raise their monitors off their desks to give themselves room to put their feet up. They bought an indoor basketball hoop that they'd always wanted for no good reason.

And do you know what? On Tuesday they went bust!

No. Just kidding.

This is a business book and that was a case study and I wouldn't have told you it if there hadn't been a significant turn around of this company's fortunes. But why did that happen?

Psychologists will tell you about the effects of colour, space and lighting on productivity. We could add that research has shown that just about any sort of change to routine produces at least a temporary increase in morale. But other things were going on there. The hands-on approach – design your own space, paint your own space, go out and shop for your own things – was important. It might also have been predictable given the research. But other benefits were an unexpected bonus.

But what about the improvement in relationships? Maybe we can become bored with communication in the same way that we can get bored with wallpaper – not so much with the people around us as with what we have to talk about and how we talk about it. And the sorts of interactions you have when you paint a wall with someone are of a refreshingly different order from the interactions you have with that same person 'at work'. It creates new opportunities for discovering and sharing. I suspect this is similar to what causes training course participants to report that the greatest benefit was talking in the hotel bar afterwards.

If you can't repaint the office, how could you introduce a similar change from the normal routine?

S is also for...

Spies

Encourage your people to be spies. Get them to talk about other companies, either through advertising they have seen and its implications, or through what they have heard from their friends and neighbours about the companies that they work for. This will:

1. Discourage a 'the grass is always greener on the other side' mentality.

2. Be a source for ideas for improving productivity and benchmarking.

3. Encourage them to be proud of their own company's developments.

4. Break down the barriers between life and work. They can talk excitedly about work in the pub rather than just bitch about it.

Make your people the radars of your organization and give them the antennae to be sensitive to change.

The use of antennae is a metaphor, although remarkably good ones can be mimed by putting your index fingers on either side of your forehead and wiggling them about.

S is also for...

Stop

> # WARNING:
> # This is the most extreme
> # exercise in this book.

It is designed for heads of companies only, since others might get into trouble.

In fact even the heads of companies would get into trouble on this one.

So don't worry. This is the exercise that no one will do...[54]

---

[54]But you could do it as a mental fire-drill...

Stop Start

The 'Stop' Exercise

How to do it:

STEP 1

Make arrangements for all the computers to go down, all the telephones, fax machines and telexes to disconnect, at 8 a.m. tomorrow morning for half a day. Don't tell anyone what you have done.

STEP 2

Turn up tomorrow morning along with everyone else.

Watch.

STEP 3

The next day, tell everybody what you learned.

Look out for the following:

1. Feel that surge of excitement when people realize that the computers are not going to come back on. When was the last time your people shared such an intensity of feeling?

2. Listen to what people talk about when they don't have to, or can't, carry out their work. How do they interact when the routine is broken, as opposed to putting on the familiar show of hard labour for your benefit?

3. How do people help those who have to complete a task? What solutions do they create? What team-working skills do they demonstrate?

S is also for...

Stress _{See} **W is for When it all gets too much**

is for

Thanks

Time Free-Fall

Trust

T is for...

Thanks

It should be the first word out of your mouth in return for a job well done – actually for any job done at all – because it cements a culture of motivation, achievement, reward and development. But it is surprising how rarely it is heard – said with **sincerity** and **eye-contact** – in the workplace. If you think you say 'Thank you' frequently, try this exercise. Next time somebody drops a report down in front of you, wait for them to get six or seven paces away from your desk, then call them back, look them in the eye and say 'Thank you'. That slight discomfort in the air is a sign of something new happening – as when first time lovers say 'I love you'.

It means that you haven't been meaning 'Thank you' much at all.

'Thanks' should be the operative word in your service department. Oh, what the hell, it should be the operative word in your whole organization.

We are very bad at saying 'Thanks', particularly when someone has just criticized us.

Come to think of it, we are even worse at doing the criticizing. You've been there. You are asked by a colleague to have a look at a presentation he has just prepared. And it stinks. And what do you say?

- 'That was bloody awful! Jesus, you need help quick...Here's at least ten good ideas which will make it better and help you knock their socks off!!'

No, you don't. You squirm with embarrassment and say, in a weak, slimy, cowardly voice:

- 'Mmm. No, it's fine. Really.'

Tsk, tsk. Shame on you. And because of that, your colleague never improves.

(See also **H is for Honesty.**)

It's the same with service. If a customer criticizes us, we should be slapping her on the back and saying:

- 'Thanks.'

or rather

- 'T.I.F.I.'

Thanks Again

What? T.I.F.I.? Yes, T.I.F.I. It stands for 'Thanks, I'll fix it':

THANKS The fundamental attitude of mind that must become the company battle cry – because receiving criticism is good, a measure of the criticizer's will to see you improve. It's a chance to make things better. How often is the real problem that we just hate being criticized? We must learn the value of 'Thanks'.

I'LL Because the customer (internal or external) needs assurance that somebody will own the problem until it is fixed. If the problem falls to someone else and you can't own it, then own the customer. This is the guarantee of the human face to your company.

FIX It must be fixed; what does it take? Ask the customer: 'What would put this right?' and, armed with the answer, do it! Fix is about going the extra mile for your customer on the safe assumption that one of your competitors will if you don't.

IT Take care what you are fixing. The problem is going to be at least in two parts: the proverbial broken kettle and the perception of your company or you now that the kettle has broken. It would be dangerous to fix the first and not the second. The customer may in fact be wrong about the kettle (they aren't always right), but there is still a negative perception that needs to be fixed. Keep talking to the customer and listen.

T.I.F.I. is a prescription for turning complaints and criticisms into a winning edge, whether you are talking about the customer service department, or whether you are talking about the day-to-day transactions within your teams.

It replaces a worthless and misplaced shame at perceived weakness into a celebration of our potential for constant improvement.

Encourage your people to be thirsty for improvement!

T is also for...

Time Free-Fall

The horrible feeling you experience when you realize that you don't have enough time to work out how to operate your video recorder or to programme 100 numbers into the memory of your mobile phone. Also the awe you feel about the lives of those who do seem to find the time to do these things.

More seriously, time free-fall is that sensation we all have in this crazy age that time is moving by too quickly or at least in such a way that we are not using it wisely. We feel that we are always missing something. We feel that we are neglecting something important. We feel that we are not achieving our objectives. Sometimes we feel that we have forgotten what our objectives were in the first place.

No time-management training will ever make us able to achieve every task – there is always too much to do. If we measure our daily success in terms of items ticked off a 'To Do' list, therefore, we are dooming ourselves to frustration (not to mention failure). Such frustration makes us quick to blame, and to concentrate only on

- what went wrong
- what other people did that hindered us.

Such negativity will make it difficult for us to find fun in our lives or in our work. Remember fun is a process, not a reward.

In order to pull the parachute on time free-fall, we need to shift the focus away from life's ever-expanding 'To Do' list.

So in your personal end-of-day process review, reflect on two areas:

THE DAY JUST GONE
- What have I done today that I can be proud of?
- What have I done today that is a good expression of what is important to me?

THE DAY TO COME
I will suppose that at least ten per cent of tomorrow is for me and for me alone and that I can use that time to do something that is important to me (in that no one is expecting, or requiring, or waiting for me to do it).

Time Free-Fall Sustained

What will I do with that time? How will I do it?

This will be more urgent and more important than anything else.

I will plan this time with all the skills that I would apply to a project at work.

Concentrating on these aspects of our lives pins down a sense that something in every day is important and achievable – that in these areas at least, we are not missing out. We can try then to learn to look forward to our time and be thankful for it, rather than curse its passing.

T is also for...

Trust

Trust me!

Sylvester to Tweety Pie

Perhaps the strongest recurring theme in this book is that of trust. Trust is the thing – perhaps, ultimately, the only thing – that binds us together.

I heard Tony Brewer of the IT Management Programme, in a seminar called 'Managing Continuous Change', ask his audience to imagine that they were a rugby team. Then he went on:

> **SCENARIO ONE:** You are the England First Fifteen, training on Wednesday night for the forthcoming rugby match at Twickenham against France. What do you talk about?

> **SCENARIO TWO:** You are the England First Fifteen, training on Wednesday night for the forthcoming rugby match at Twickenham. But you don't know who you'll be playing. What do you talk about?

> **SCENARIO THREE:** You are the England First Fifteen, training on Wednesday night for a forthcoming rugby match. But you don't know who you'll be playing, or where, or even when. What do you talk about?

> **SCENARIO FOUR:** You have gathered for training on Wednesday night for a forthcoming match. But you don't know who you'll be playing, or where, or when. And, worse than that, you don't even know what game you'll be playing. What do you talk about?

When things change and become increasingly difficult, strange and unpredictable, when that roller-coaster is cranking up to the top of what seems an unfeasibly steep hill, our faith in competence and measurement deserts us. The tactics we practised in rugby training are useless against the unknown. We are left with trust. We trust that our team mates will be there with us. We trust in team spirit, and faith, and values, and principles. We trust that those things we promised each other when times were easier will still hold true now that times are hard.

Trust Another

In terms of some of the ideas in this book, for example, we trust that we are still free to fail, even though the budget is tight. We trust that asking for help is still seen as a sign of strength, even when the person we are asking is busy. We trust that we are still able to smile, even when the work is serious. We trust that we are still able to take a walk in the park, even when the deadline appears to be looming. We trust that we are still able to join in with energy and passion, even though the work is repetitive.

And like many of the ideas in this book, trust cannot be imposed or installed, like a new word-processing system. It cannot be demanded as a new company standard in a company-wide memo.

Trust is measured by actions, but it comes from within. We should be justifiably angry when trust is broken because a person's actions do not live up to what he or she promised. And every time we make a promise, every time we put ourselves into a position where we are trusted, we do not just make a social contract. We make a personal one too. If we fail our colleague, we can make excuses. It is less easy to fool ourselves.

I believe that we do not have an unlimited number of 'personal trust contracts' to break. Some managers spend years trying to fix broken trust. Sometimes, whole companies cannot recover.

If we make promises to ourselves and break them, then we replace that capacity for trustworthiness with the certainty of doubt. We may not display that doubt to others, but it is there, and it will weaken our will and sense of possibility.

If, on the other hand, we keep promises, we begin to fill up that capacity for trustworthiness. This strengthens our ability – in others' eyes and in our own.

Trust Yet Another

How can you be sure that you are trusted? You will have to have this answered on both the social and personal levels.

Ask yourself if you are trustworthy – how many times have you known yourself to break a promise – social or personal? There may have been times when nobody actually noticed, or when you were able to cover up the consequences of your actions. But you will have known. You can't kid me, or you.

Then ask your colleagues. And ask often. Research at Ohio State University in 1988 found that trust was about as precious and fragile as a Ming vase. In tests, trust was found to last 0.00000021 seconds after the act that broke it.

How do you build trust? Give something away – something that can be used against you. If you don't do this, they'll know that you don't trust them – and they'll be right. And anyway, how else can you find out if they are worth trusting in the first place?

U

is for

Urinals

U is for...

Urinals

As my dear mother always used to say: piss in the same urinals.

Now what she meant by that she was never able to say, because she never shook off the debilitating side-effects of the treatment she was on at the time.

But if she had ever been called up, Tom Peters-like, to talk at $20,000 per hour in front of a roomful of gormless, starched, over-bonused chief executives who couldn't even thrive on chaos if it sneaked up behind them and put a potato in the exhaust pipe of their company Mercedes, I think she probably would have said something like this:

> 'Piss in the same urinals, boys and girls. They used to call it Management by Walking About – MBWA. Now it's PITSU. It means get down there and talk to people. Listen. Learn. For those of you who have never seen a urinal, don't feel excluded. What I mean is don't be aloof. Don't hide in the executive boardroom. Don't park in the executive car parking space. Don't have your own dining room. Move about. Move amongst. And above all, don't be a stranger...

And I think that she would have had a point.

is for

Vertigo

Vitality

V is for...

Vertigo

This is the horrible, light-headed, disorienting feeling that you'll have when you start to implement some of the ideas in this book.

Sometimes it will feel like fear because you will be controlling less and doing more. Sometimes it will feel like embarrassment, because you'll be having to say things like 'Thank you,' and 'Sorry' because, and as if, you mean them. And much of the time it will feel like anger and cynicism, because people are slow to change, unwilling to take the initiative, reluctant to stick their head above the parapet, scared to trust you.

Be brave. You are reacting against a whole society's idea of what organizations are for and how we are all supposed to be at work. Don't stop.

There is no finish line.

The Nike Corporation

A Message to my Son...
on the Eve of his First Job

I looked on all the labour that I had laboured to do, and behold, all was vanity and a striving after wind.

Ecclesiastes

...but I was so much older then, I'm younger than that now...

Bob Dylan

'Well, son, the book didn't work, so it'll be hell tomorrow. But never mind, you'll be out soon enough. Give it a try for Dad, eh?

Some of my colleagues who've just retired say some things to me that make me think. They're not revolutionaries. They've done it, they've reached the top, they've been successful and now they tell me what they've finally realized.

And they're not saying "Hey, I understand now! What I actually should have done is fire people better!"

They're saying, "I had to put up with a lot of non-fun. I had to put up with playing a game which was sustained by fear and inertia. I railed against it where I could. But to tell you the truth, as I look back on it, I feel a bit cheated. I wish I could have my time again."

They're right.

Don't cheat yourself, son.'

V is also for...

Vitality

It's what we need in these crazy, roller-coaster nineties.

It is what you'll develop if you challenge everybody to become **involved**, openly **sharing information**, by asking questions and listening, to perform **constantly improving processes** in a culture of **feedback, honesty and fun**.

Imagine that your company is hooked up to a life-support system. That electronic blip is still hopping across the monitor (just), but what are the vital signs?

Is the heart pumping?

- How freely does information flow?
- Does it travel right down to the extremities?

Is the blood still healthy?

- Is the information useful to, or even understood by, those who need it?
- Do we taint it with fruitless gossip and rumour-mongering because we are too scared to speak up?
- Do we tell the truth?

Is the brain functioning?

- Are our analytical skills balanced by our ability to dream?

Do we still have opposable thumbs?

- When we pick up a task, do we run with it?

Have we still got balls?

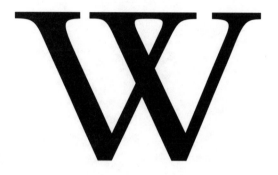

is for

Walt Disney

When it all gets too much...

W is for...

Walt Disney

'When you wish upon a star –
makes no difference who you are –
anything your heart desires
will come to you.

If your heart is in your dreams
no request is too extreme,
when you wish upon a star,
as dreamers do.

Like a bolt out of the blue
fate steps in and sees you through.
When you wish upon a star
your dreams come true'

Great, huh?
I bet a lot of you folks don't believe that.

Jiminy Cricket, *Pinnochio*

*I prefer to entertain people in the hope that they learn
rather than teach people in the hope that they are entertained.*

Walt Disney

Get a life

The official Walt Disney Corporation statement in response to press accusations that *The Lion King* is racist and sexist and homophobic and animalist and speciesist and genderist and heightest and generally responsible for the ills of the world.

Q: *What's the difference between Bing Crosby and Walt Disney?*

A: *Bing sings and Walt Disney.*

A joke

W is also for...

When it all gets too much...

A FIRST-AID KIT

1. Relax...relax....relax...relax.

2. See things in perspective; be positive.

3. Name your fear ('Michael' is a good name to use).

4. Smile (think of something funny).

5. Listen to your breathing.

6. Relax your eye muscles.

7. Smile again. Look up. Stand up.

8. Loosen your shoulders and neck.

9. Clench and release tension in your hands.

10. Take your time.

11. Forget it and get on with your life.

When it's still all too much...

It is quickly apparent that the majority of the prescriptions and medicines in this kit are physical ones. They are to do with making adjustments to your body, not your mind. Stress is an emotional reaction to the perception that there are too many demands on too few resources, but the etymology of the word 'emotion' gives us an indication of its root causes. Emotion is from the Latin prefix *e* meaning from and the past participle of the verb *movere* meaning 'to move'. Our emotions are affected by the way we move. If you assume the position of a depressed person – head down, shoulders hunched, brow furrowed, shallow breathing – your brain will adjust itself to a suitable alignment with that physical shape, i.e. it will begin to emit feelings of depression.

In the same way, it is extremely difficult to feel unhappy when you are standing erect, with shoulders back and a smile on your face. The First-Aid Kit concentrates on releasing tension in the physical body (the concrete and easily adjusted aspect of our existence) to help prevent negative emotions, thoughts and feelings (abstract and more difficult to budge) controlling our minds. We have nothing to fear but our fear. The human mind is capable of unleashing horrible imaginings that are quite real to the body, imaginings that tell the body to prepare for a catastrophe that will never happen. Don't let it. Get your body into the right shape for a stress-free life at work.

XYZ

is for

erm...

XYZ is for...

erm...

oo, erm...

All right, even the simplest of structures fall down sometimes.
This is the interactive part of the book.
Do XYZ yourself. (See **E is for Empowerment.**)

Another

1. Tell someone that you'd like to introduce some more fun into work. You'll be surprised how people will open up and give you ideas or at least stop you believing that you are alone or mad.

2. Perform some emotional aerobics — see if becoming passionate about something can make you tired.

3. Visualize a new life, a new job. Take a sabbatical from your current surroundings.

4. Remember that the most successful innovators know more about failure than they do about success. Forgive yourself.

5. Draw a cartoon of the person you hate most at work.

6. Go to the shop, buy a postcard and send it to yourself. You'll receive it tomorrow. What would you write?

7. Do something nice for somebody for no good reason at all.

8. On the way to work: take a moment to assess your weekend or evening. What went well? What can you decide to try and bring to work with you? Your ability to relax? Your ability to tease or laugh? Your confidence in yourself? And what can you decide to leave behind? What moods or worries, however valid and unavoidable, will hamper you in your work? Save your energies to deal with these when you have the time to concentrate on them. Don't dissipate your energies by focusing on things that you know you cannot deal with whilst at work, however much you worry.

Things

9. **On the way from work:**

   (a) If you need to work at home or during the journey home, be realistic: pack in your briefcase only the amount of work that you can possibly complete in the short time you have. Don't allow your ego to make a liar of you. Complete what you set out to achieve and you will be rewarded by success. Heaving around a briefcase bulging with paperwork which you will never complete might impress your boss but will eventually guarantee you a home time characterized by frustration, guilt and fear. Have a look in your case now: how many pieces of paper in there have travelled enough miles to qualify for a frequent traveller discount?

   (b) Deliberately walk a few paces slower than the crowd, drive a few miles per hour slower than the rest (I know this is difficult in a traffic jam). It is easy to be drawn into the dazed, lemming-like surge of the human commuter group which is less about efficiency of travel and more about the communal programming of stress. Try taking a few minutes to observe a main line station from above; watch how the commuters stream around from platform to platform; then quietly say to yourself the word 'lemmings'.

   (c) OK so today, work wasn't fun. It was horrible. It was an absolute nightmare. In this case, you need to make a formal or symbolic separation from your work: when you reach your doorstep, or are back in your driveway: PAUSE – BREATHE – RELAX. Don't rush through the door in your desire to 'be home' to find you have

   continued overleaf...

Another Ten Things

that you can do starting tomorrow to introduce some life into work:

from previous page...

> inadvertently introduced all the tension and fatigue from the office. If you bottle stress up, it'll kill you. If you take it out on your partner or kids, it will kill your relationship. This is difficult, but it needs to be addressed. Talk to your spouse about these moments — is their joy at seeing you again tempered by fear that you may be uncontrollably moody? What ideas can you think of together to smooth the transition from 'work' into 'home'?

> (d) OK so last night wasn't fun. It was horrible. It was an absolute nightmare. You had a blazing row. PAUSE. BREATHE. RELAX. Don't take it to work.

10. Make a decision to be as proud of your life as you try to be proud of your career. Project management, financial planning, management of scarce resources, communication, negotiation, facilities management, strategy and forecasting — you do all these just to live. And you are these too: emotional investor, sexual athlete, progenitor, entertainer, and so on, and so on.

It's a hard life.

A Survival Pack

To take with you on your quest to introduce some life into work:

Books and Magazines

- Any collection of urban myths
- Any Gary Larson collection
- *The Tao of Pooh*
- *Maverick!* by Ricardo Semler
- *Liberation Management* and *Thriving on Chaos* by Tom Peters
- A book about something which you studied at school, college or university that you enjoyed but never thought would have any use in business. (It just might.)
- A thesaurus (or some alternative glossary, lexicon or listing of synonyms)
- A book of quotations
- A book of poetry
- A copy of your relevant trade magazine or professional journal
- The *Harvard Business Review*
- *Psychology Today*
- *Private Eye*, *Viz*, *Stamps and Stamping*, or whatever makes you laugh

Objects

- Whiteboard
- Pack of Post-it Notes for you to leave happy KITs (Keep In Touch) on other people's desks
- Stress reliever: e.g. a brightly-coloured small foam ball to throw against the walls
- Taiwanese toy that makes a ridiculous noise
- Good selection of silly symbols or pictures
- File of funny, wise or provocative articles or cartoons that you've collected or found or stolen
- Enough money to provide a regular supply of tea
- Some sweets
- Hat

Counsellor: *Well, do you have any idea of what you want to do?*

Anchovy: *Yes, yes I have.*

Counsellor: *What?*

Anchovy: *Lion taming...*

Counsellor: *Fine, fine. But do you, do you have any qualifications?*

Anchovy: *Yes, I've got a hat.*

Counsellor: *A hat?*

Anchovy: *Yes, a hat. A lion taming hat. A hat with 'lion tamer' on it.*

The Vocational Guidance Counsellor Sketch,
Monty Python's Flying Circus

Epilogue

What we call the beginning is often the end
And to make an end is to make a beginning.
The end is where we start from.

Four Quartets: *Little Gidding*, T.S. Eliot

So here we are at the end of a book called *How to Make Work* FUN!

You'll have noted by now, and with some relief, that this is not a book about jokes and parties. This book is not a licence for the office wag, heaven forbid. In fact I don't actually explain how to have fun, because I think fun is what you have when it feels as if nothing is stopping you. So it's a book about taking down the barriers. And that is what is called the Paradox of Intent.

Fun at any price? No. There are many workforces which are driven by their attitude to threatening or unstable situations which in turn produce emotions such as disappointment, anger and frustration. How can we ask a company on the verge of takeover to behave like a troupe of clowns? Work, like life, has (must have) its balance of pain and pleasure (see D is for Dissatisfaction).

So I do not look on people at work as a delicate bunch who can only operate with a smile on their face – that eerie expression of stupefied contentment sometimes used by politicians or brought about in people on Quaaludes. In work I want life, with its full span of emotion, expression and experience, not some happy veneer of life. Forcing 'all the best bits' from life into work would be as bad as the present situation we've got now – many of the worst bits.

Fun is what happens when you feel that nothing (apart from the laws of the land and a moderate sense of decency) is stopping you from having it. Ask some of your colleagues what they thought was fun over the last six months and you'll arrive with a list like this (I did):

- Walking the Lyke Wake walk in November (a 125-mile stretch of Yorkshire moorland).
- Raising £1000 for charity in a sponsored bicycle race.
- Changing a tyre in the snow in Oregon.
- Discovering how to fillet a fish.
- Finishing a round of golf after the darkness had made the ball invisible.
- Transporting a heavily-in-labour wife to hospital for the delivery.
- Working through the night to compose an advertising jingle for a cold cure.
- Playing in the ladies' football team at the local church.

No balloons, no custard pies

See, Mr and Mrs Straitjacket? Human beings are not latent imbeciles. But they do have a range of experiences and hopes and values and a pressing need for growth and development and participation and respect and morality and meaning and happiness – and these are areas which our organizations have hardly begun to tap.

We end with the realization that perhaps work is like fun, if not yet fun. Fun is certainly like work, in that, at the same time, it is both a personal and a social experience. Whatever fun is, it seems:

- it's fun if you can enjoy it (personal)

and/or

- it's fun if you are with people you like (social).

To make work fun, then, we need to extend the ways that we can find enjoyment in the whole experience of being at work; whether it be in the way we talk about work, the way we think about work, the way we do the work or the way in which we create the environments in which we work. And then we need to improve our proficiency at being social – our ability to make people like us, and our capacity for finding things to like in other people.

Only when people can begin to experience more of these inspirations at work are they going to be truly motivated to be there. If they could express these things at work they might feel less like leaving at 5 p.m. They might even want to come back tomorrow.

And think what that might do for the bottom line.

So

this

is

Goodbye.

No.
Goodbye is Goodbye.

This is this.

An Invitation

To all who read and enjoy this book you are cordially invited to help me bring life into work, and work to life.

If you want:

• To see what fun could do for your organization, regardless of your level or job title, but don't know how or where to start

• To exchange war stories of fun or funless environments

• To communicate with kindred spirits on the 'fun at work' network

• To hear a great joke

Get in touch.

If today you have:

• Cheered someone up

• Relieved someone's stress

• Developed someone's potential

• Blown someone's trumpet

• Deflated someone's balloon.

In short, if you have made someone's life at work a little bit better, don't hide it, share it. Someone else may want to try it.

You can write to me at:

David Firth
How To Make Work Fun
PO Box 4734
London SE23 32A

R.S.V.P.   Dress: Loud Tie